Hans H. Ørberg

LINGVA
LATINA
PER SE ILLVSTRATA

M000296942

Latine Disco
Student's Manual

LINGVA LATINA
PER SE ILLVSTRATA

Pars I:
Familia Romana (978-1-58510-201-3); hard cover (978-1-58510-238-5)
Latine Disco: Student's Manual (978-1-58510-050-7)
Grammatica Latina (978-1-58510-223-5)
Exercitia Latina I (978-1-58510-212-9)
Latin-English Vocabulary (978-1-58510-049-1)
Lingva Latina: Familia Romana CD-ROM for PC (87-90696-08-5)
Exercitia Latina I CD-ROM for PC (978-87-90696-10-8)

Pars II:
Roma Aeterna (978-1-58510-233-4); hardcover (978-1-58510-314-0)
Exercitia Latina II (978-1-58510-067-5)
Indices (87-997016-9-3)
Instructions for Part II (978-1-58510-055-2)
Latin-English Vocabulary (978-1-58510-052-1)
Lingva Latina: Roma Aeterna CD-ROM For PC (87-90696-09-3)
Exercitia Latina II CD-ROM for PC (978-87-90696-12-2)

Ancillaries:
CD-ROM for Mac, contains Familia Romana, Roma Aeterna, Exercitia Latina I & II (978-87-90696-13-9)
Caesaris: Commentarii De Bello Gallico (87-90696-06-9)
Colloqvia Personarvm (978-1-58510-156-6)
Menaechmi ex Plavti Comoedia (1-58510-051-X)
P. Vergilii Maronis: Aeneis, Libros I et IV (978-87-90696-17-7)
Petronivs: Cena Trimalchionis (87-90696-04-2)
Plavtus: Amphitryo (87-997016-7-7)
Sallustius & Cicero: Catilina (87-90696-11-5)
Sermones Romani (97-90696-07-7)

For College Students:
Lingva Latina: A College Companion (978-1-58510-191-7)

For further information on the complete series and new titles,
visit www.pullins.com.

CONTENTS

Introduction .... p. 3
Instructions
Chapter 1 9
Chapter 2 11
Chapter 3 12
Chapter 4 14
Chapter 5 15
Chapter 6 16
Chapter 7 17
Chapter 8 18
Chapter 9 19
Chapter 10 20
Chapter 11 21
Chapter 12 22
Chapter 13 23
Chapter 14 25
Chapter 15 26
Chapter 16 27
Chapter 17 28
Chapter 18 29
Chapter 19 30
Chapter 20 31
Chapter 21 32
Chapter 22 34
Chapter 23 35
Chapter 24 36
Chapter 25 37
Chapter 26 38
Chapter 27 39
Chapter 28 40
Chapter 29 41
Chapter 30 42
Chapter 31 43
Chapter 32 44
Chapter 33 45
Chapter 34 46
Chapter 35 48
Index 49

INTRODUCTION

LINGVA LATINA, the Latin Language

The Latin language, *lingua Latīna,* was the language of the *Latīnī,* the inhabitants of *Latium,* a region of central Italy, including the city of Rome (*Rōma*), which according to tradition had been founded by *Rōmulus* in 753 B.C. In the following centuries the dominion of Rome, *imperium Rōmānum,* spread over the whole of Italy, and from there over the Western and Eastern Mediterranean. By the 2nd century A.D. the Roman emperor ruled most of Europe, North Africa, and the Near and Middle East. In the Western European provinces, *Hispānia, Gallia, Britannia, Germānia* (Southern Germany), and in the Balkans, e.g. in *Dācia* (Romania), the Latin language spread rapidly. In Greece and in the Eastern provinces Greek maintained its dominant position, so that the ancients had two world languages, Greek and Latin.

Latin, the language of Latium

the language of the Roman Empire

After the fall of the Western Empire Latin was supplanted as a spoken language in some of the border provinces, e.g. Britain and Africa; in the other provinces spoken Latin developed into the *Romance* languages, e.g. Italian, French, Spanish, Portuguese, and Romanian.

the Romance languages

Today Latin is nobody's mother tongue. That is why it is called a 'dead' language. However, this is rather a misleading term. For centuries Latin was just as much a living language in the vast Roman empire as English is today in the English-speaking world. And this 'dead' language had such vitality that throughout the Middle Ages it remained unchallenged as the common language of the educated classes of Europe. Up to the 18th century Latin retained its leadership as the medium of international scholarship. In our own day the classical language survives in the Roman Catholic Church, and most scientific terms are still Latin.

the cultural language of Europe

As a result of the position of Latin as the international cultural language, the national European languages have been enriched with large numbers of Latin words. Apart from the Romance languages, where non-Latin words are exceptions, English is the language which has absorbed by far the greatest number of Latin words. Indeed more than half of the English vocabulary is directly or indirectly derived from Latin.

Latin words in English

3

Orthography and Pronunciation

The Latin alphabet had 23 letters: A B C D E F G H I K L M N O P Q R S T V X Y Z (K was hardly used, Y and Z only in Greek words). The small letters are a later development of these capital letters. The characters J, U and W were unknown: I and V denoted the vowels *i* and *u* as well as the consonants *j* and *v* (pronounced like English *y* and *w*). Not until the 16th century was the distinction between the characters *I i and J j* and between *V v* and *U u* observed. In our Latin books we do not use *J j*, but we distinguish the consonants *V v* from the vowels *U u*, except in titles that are written in capital letters, e.g. CAPITVLVM, IVLIVS.

It is possible to determine, with a high degree of accuracy, how the Latin words were pronounced in ancient times. The main types of evidence are the following:

(1) Latin orthography, especially variations form the norm.

(2) The pronunciation of the Romance languages, which represent the later development of spoken Latin.

(3) Statements about the pronunciation found in the writings of ancient Latin grammarians and other authors.

(4) The representation of Latin words in other languages.

On the basis of such sources of information we can lay down the main rules governing the pronunciation of Latin in the Classical period (the first century B.C.) as follows:

Vowels

vowels:
short: *a e i o u y*
long: *ā ē ī ō ū ȳ*

A clear distinction was made in pronunciation, but not in writing, between long and short vowels. In LINGVA LATINA every long vowel is marked with a macron [¯]: *ā, ē, ī, ō, ū, ȳ*; consequently the absence of a macron shows that the vowel is short: *a, e, i, o, u, y*.

Short vowels	Long vowels
a as the first *a* in 'aha': *amat*	*ā* as in 'father': *ālā, pānis*
e as in 'let': *et, bene*	*ē* as in Scottish 'late' (no diphthong!): *mē*
i as in 'fit': *in, nimis*	*ī* as *ee* in 'feet': *hīc, līberī*
o as in 'hot': *post, modo*	*ō* as in Scottish 'go' (no diphthong!): *pōnō*
u as in 'full': *num, sumus*	*ū* as in 'fool': *ūna, tū*
y as French *u* in 'lune': *Syria*	*ȳ* as French *u* in 'pur': *Lȳdia*

Diphthongs

A diphthong is a combination of two vowels in one syllable. The Latin diphthongs are: *ae, oe, au, eu, ui*.

ae as *ie* in 'die': *Graecia, laetus, paene.*
oe as *oi* in 'boil': *foedus, poena.*
au as *ou* in 'loud': *aut, nauta.*
eu as *e+u* combined into one syllable: *Eurōpa, heu, heus, neu, seu*. (But the endings *-us, -um, -unt* form separate syllables after *e*: *de|us, me|us, e|um, e|unt, aure|us*.)
ui in *cui, huic, cuius, huius* as *u+i* combined into one syllable.

4

Consonants

b as in English: *bibit, ab.* (But *bs* and *bt* as *ps* and *pt: absunt, obtulit*).

c always hard as in 'cat' (= *k*, without aspiration): *canis, centum, circus, nec.*

ch, ph, th as *k, p, t* with aspiration: *pulcher, amphitheātrum.*

d as in English: *dē, dedit, ad.*

f as in English: *forum, flūmen.*

g as in English 'get' (never as in 'gem'): *gallus, gemma, agit.*

gn as *ngn* in 'willingness': *signum, pugna, magnus.*

h as in English [tending to disappear]: *hīc, homō, nihil.*

l as in English: *lūna, gladius, male, vel.*

m as in English: *mē, domus, tam.* [In the unstressed endings -*am*, -*em*, -*um* it tended to disappear.]

n as in English: *nōn, ūnus;* before *c, g, q* as in 'ink': *incola, longus, quīnque.* [Before *s* it tended to disappear: *mēnsa, īnsula.*]

p as in English (without aspiration): *pēs, populus, prope.*

ph as English *p* with aspiration: see above under *ch.*

qu as English *qu* in 'quick': *quis, aqua, equus.*

r rolled (as in Scottish and in Italian and Spanish): *rēs, ōra, arbor, cūr.*

s as in English 'gas' (never voiced as in 'has'): *sē, rosa, is.*

t as in English (without aspiration): *tē, ita, et.*

th as English *t* with aspiration: see above under *ch.*

v as English *w: vōs, vīvus.*

x as in English (= *cs*): *ex, saxum.*

z as English *z* in 'zone': *zōna*

i consonant, as English *y* in 'yet', before a vowel at the beginning of a word (or preceded by a prefix) and between vowels: *iam, iubēre, con-iungere, eius.*

u consonant, as English *w*, in the combination *ngu* before a vowel and sometimes in the combination *su* before *ā* and *ē: lingua, sanguis, suādēre, suāvis, cōnsuētūdō.*

Double consonants were held longer than single consonants (as in 'thinness', 'roommate', 'rattail'): *ille, annus, nummus, terra, ecce, littera, oppidum.* [The *i* consonant between vowels was pronounced double: *eius* as *eiius, maior* as *maiior*, in LINGVA LATINA written *māior.*]

Late Latin pronunciation

The Classical Latin pronunciation described above was that of educated Romans in the first century B.C. In imperial times (1st–5th centuries A.D.) the pronunciation of Latin underwent considerable changes. The most conspicuous are the following:

(1) The dipthongs *ae* and *oe* were simplified into long *ē* (an open vowel).

(2) *v* was pronounced like English *v.*

(3) *ph* was pronounced like *f, th* like *t*, and *ch* like *c* (= *k*).

(4) *ti* before a vowel became *tsi* (except after *s, t, x*).

(5) The distinction between long and short vowels was obscured, as short vowels at the end of a stressed syllable became long (open vowels), and long vowels in unstressed syllables became short.

(6) Finally (in the 5th century) the pronunciation of *c* and *g* changed before the front vowels *e, i, y, ae, oe: c* came to be pronounced like English *ch* in 'chin' (*sc*, however, like *sh*) and *g* (and *i* consonant) like English *g* in 'gin' or *j* in 'jam'. Outside of Italy *c* in this position was pronounced *ts.*

consonants:
b c d f g h k l m n p q r s t x z i v (u)

double consonants

Late Latin pronunciation

5

the *Italian* or *Ecclesiastical* pronunciation	The main features of this Late Latin pronunciation survive in the pronunciation of Latin still used in Italy. This 'Italian' pronunciation of Latin is widely used in the Roman Catholic Church and in church singing.
	The Classical Latin pronunciation is now generally taught in British and American schools; but this dates only from the beginning of the 20th century. Before then most English-speaking people pronounced Latin words as if they were English. This traditional English pronunciation of Latin is still alive: it is used in the English forms of Latin names (*Plautus, Cicero, Scipio, Caesar, Augustus,* etc.) and in a great many Latin words and phrases in current use in English (e.g. *radius, medium, area, status quo, et cetera, ad infinitum, bona fide, vice versa,* etc.).
the *traditional English* pronunciation	

Syllabic division

division into syllables — Words are divided into syllables in Latin according to the following simple rules:

(1) A single consonant goes with the following vowel: *do-mi-nus, o-cu-lus, cu-bi-cu-lum, pe-te-re.*

(2) When two or more consonants follow a vowel, the last consonant is carried over to the next syllable: *Sep-tem-ber, tem-pes-tās, pis-cis, con-iūnc-tus.* Exception: *b, d, g, p, t, c* and *f* are not separated from a following *r* or *l* (except sometimes in poetry): *li-brī, sa-cra, pa-tri-a, cas-tra, tem-plum in-te-gra, ce-re-brum.*

Note: The digraphs *ch, ph, th* and *qu* count as single consonants and are not separated: *pul-cher, am-phi-the-ā-trum, a-li-quis;* and *x,* as representing two consonants (*cs*), is not separated from the preceding vowel: *sax-um, dīx-it.* Compounds should be divided into components: *ad-est, ab-est, trāns-it.*

Accentuation

accent or stress — In words of two syllables the accent (stress) is always on the first syllable: *'ubi, 'multī, 'valē, 'erant, 'leō.*

two possibilities:
(1) the *penultimate,* or
(2) the *antepenultimate* — In words of more than two syllables there are two possibilities: the accent falls on (1) the last syllable but one, the *penultimate,* or (2) the last syllable but two, the *antepenultimate.* The basic rule is this:

> The *penultimate* is accented unless it ends in a *short vowel,* in which case the *antepenultimate* is accented.

look at the *penultimate* (last but one) syllable! — Accordingly, to determine the position of the accent in a Latin word, look at the *penultimate* (the last but one syllable):

The penultimate is *accented* when it ends
(a) in a *long vowel* or diphthong: *La'tīna, vi'dēre, a'mīca, Rō'mānus, ō'rātor, per'sōna, a'moena;* or
(b) in a *consonant: se'cunda, vī'gintī, lī'bertās, co'lumna, ma'gister.*

If it ends (c) in a *short vowel,* the penultimate is *unaccented* and the accent falls on the preceding syllable, the *antepenultimate: 'īnsula, 'fēmina, 'patria, 'oppidum, 'improbus, dī'videre, in'terrogat, ō'ceanus, 'persequī, 'cerebrum.*

LINGVA LATINA, the Latin course

The Latin course LINGVA LATINA PER SE ILLVSTRATA ('The Latin language illustrated by itself') consists of two parts, PARS I and II. The first part, FAMILIA ROMANA, is the fundamental course. The 35 chapters form a sequence of scenes and incidents from the life of a Roman family in the 2nd century A.D. The book is written entirely in Latin, but from beginning to end the text is so graded that every sentence is intelligible *per se*, because the meaning or function of all new words and forms is made clear by the context, or, if necessary, by pictures or marginal notes using vocabulary already learned. Thus there is no need to look up words, to analyze, or to translate in order to understand the meaning. Vocabulary and grammar are learned by the observation of a large number of illustrative examples which are part of the coherent text.

LINGVA LATINA
PER SE ILLVSTRATA
I. FAMILIA ROMANA

The *pictures* are used not only to explain words denoting material things, but also to illustrate happenings and situations. In making the pictures ancient models have been followed scrupulously: clothing, buildings, furniture etc. are reproduced as we know them to have been from archaeological finds. In this way much of the information given in the text about the conditions under which the ancient Romans lived is illustrated.

pictures

In the *marginal notes* the following signs are used:
(1) sign of equation [=] between *synonyms,* words with the same meaning, e.g. *-que = et;*
(2) sign of opposition [↔] between *antonyms,* words of opposite meanings, e.g. *sine ↔ cum;*
(3) colon [:] to show the meaning of a word in a given context, e.g. *eam : Iūliam;*
(4) sign of derivation [<] to show from what known word a new word is derived, e.g. *amor < amāre.*

marginal notes
signs:
[=] 'the same as'
[↔] 'the opposite of'
[:] 'that is', 'here:'
[<] 'derived from'

The text of each chapter is divided into two or three lessons (*lēctiōnēs,* marked by Roman numerals *I, II, III* in the margin) and followed by a section on grammar, GRAMMATICA LATINA. In this section new grammatical points introduced in the main text are recapitulated and illustrated by systematically arranged examples with the Latin grammatical terms. A survey of inflections, TABVLA DECLINATIONVM, is found on pages 307–311. A more detailed morphology is published separately (see p. 8).

lēctiōnēs: I; II; III

The three exercises, PENSVM A, B and C, at the end of each chapter serve to secure the learning of grammar and vocabulary and the understanding of the text. PENSVM A is a grammatical exercise, where the missing *endings* are to be filled in. In PENSVM B you are supposed to fill the blanks with new *words* introduced in the chapter (there is a list of the new words in the margin). PENSVM C consists of questions to be answered with short Latin *sentences.*

exercises:
PENSVM A: words
PENSVM B: endings
PENSVM C: sentences

As you progress with your reading, you will come across some words whose meaning you have forgotten. Such words should be looked up in the alphabetical word-list INDEX VOCABVLORVM at the end of the book. Here you will find a precise reference to the chapter (in bold figures) and the line of the chapter where the words occur for the first time. A reference to more than one place means that the same word occurs in more than one sense. In most cases the reading of the sentence in which the word appears is enough to help you recall the meaning. The INDEX GRAMMATICVS on pages 326-327 refers to the presentation of the grammatical forms.

INDEX VOCABVLORVM

7

Latin-English
Vocabulary I

Students who have doubts about their own ability to arrive at the exact meaning of every new word can get a *Latin-English Vocabulary I*. But this vocabulary is intended solely as a key to check the meaning of words – the careful student will not need it at all.

supplements:
GRAMMATICA LATINA,
COLLOQVIA PERSONA-
RVM
EXERCITIA LATINA I

The fundamental course has three supplements:
(1) GRAMMATICA LATINA, a Latin morphology.
(2) COLLOQVIA PERSONARVM, a collection of supplementary texts, mostly dialogue.
(3) EXERCITIA LATINA I, an extensive collection of additional exercises for each of the 133 *lēctiōnēs* in FAMILIA ROMANA.

LINGVA LATINA II: ROMA AETERNA

LINGVA LATINA
PER SE ILLVSTRATA
II. ROMA AETERNA

Part II of LINGVA LATINA, with the subtitle ROMA AETERNA ('Eternal Rome'), is the advanced course. It can be studied immediately after Part I, but it makes much heavier demands on the student. The main subject is Roman history as told by the Romans themselves, i.e. authors like Vergil, Ovid, Livy, Sallust, Cornelius Nepos, Cicero, and others. As in Part I each chapter is followed by three PENSA, which serve to recapitulate and extend grammatical knowledge, rehearse new words, and practice the rules of derivation.

INDICES

EXERCITIA LATINA II
Lat.-Engl. Vocabulary II

The INDICES volume belonging to this part contains lists of Roman consuls and their triumphs (FASTI CONSVLARES & TRIVMPHALES), a name index (INDEX NOMINVM) with short explanations in Latin, and an index of all the words used in both parts of the course. There is also a volume of EXERCITIA LATINA II for Part II, and a *Latin-English Vocabulary II* covering both parts.

follow-up editions:
Sermōnēs Rōmānī
Plautus: *Amphitryō*
Caesar: *Dē bellō Gallicō*
Petrōnius: *Cēna Trimal-
chiōnis*
Catilīna. Sallust & Cicero

After finishing Part I of LINGVA LATINA you can also go on to read the follow-up editions of Latin authors: (1) *Sermōnēs Rōmānī*, an anthology of classical texts, (2) Plautus: *Amphitryō*, and (3) Caesar: *Dē bellō Gallicō*. These abridged but otherwise unadapted editions are provided with marginal notes explaining all words not found in Part I. (4) A similar illustrated edition of Petrōnius: *Cēna Trimalchiōnis,* can be read by students who are halfway through Part II. (5) *Catilīna*, an edition of most of Sallust's *Dē coniūrātiōne Catilīnae* and Cicero's speeches *In Catilinam I* and *III*, is annotated so as to be within the reach of students who have finished Part II.

LINGVA LATINA on CD

LINGVA LATINA on CD

LINGVA LATINA Parts I and II are available on CD-ROMs with the complete text, audio-recordings, and interactive editions of the *Pensa*. The CD *Latine audio* contains a recording of chapters I–X of FAMILIA ROMANA in the restored classical pronunciation of Latin.

Instructons

The following *Instructions* provide information on key points to be noted in each chapter of Part I. It is advisable to put off reading these instructions till you have read the chapter in question, for the Latin text is designed to train you to make your own linguistic observations. The explanations given in the instructions are meant to call your attention to facts that you have already ascertained and to formulate rules of grammar that you have seen illustrated by numerous examples in the text. The instructions also teach you the international grammatical terminology, which is derived from Latin.

Instructions for Part II are published in a separate volume: LATINE DISCO II.

8

INSTRUCTIONS

Chapter 1

In the first chapter we take you almost 2000 years back into the past, to the time when the Roman Empire was at the height of its power, extending from the Atlantic Ocean to the Caspian Sea and from Scotland to the Sahara. We give you a few geographical facts as background for the sketches from life in ancient Rome which follow.

the Roman Empire

On the map of the Roman Empire facing the first page you will find all the geographical names occurring in the chapter. After locating the names *Rōma, Italia, Eurōpa, Graecia*, etc., you will understand what is said about the situation of the city of *Rōma* in the first sentence: *Rōma in Italiā est*, and about *Italia* and *Graecia* in the next two: *Italia in Eurōpā est. Graecia in Eurōpā est*. This is said once more in a single sentence: *Italia et Graecia in Eurōpā sunt*. The meaning of *et* should be quite clear, but can you tell why it is now *sunt* instead of *est*? If not, look in the margin, and read the next two sentences as well. Have you discovered when it is *est* and when *sunt*? If so, you have learned the first rule of grammar. You will gradually learn the whole of Latin grammar in this way – that is, by working out grammatical rules from your own observation of the text.

et ('......')

Did you also notice the slight difference between *Italia* and *Italiā*, and what little word produces the long *-ā*? This is pointed out in the first marginal note. – Another thing worth noticing: *est* and *sunt* come at the end of the sentence; but you will see that it is not always so, *Rōma est in Italiā* is also correct: the word order is less rigid in Latin than in English.

Italia
in Italiā

flexible word order

Is it really possible, you may ask, to understand everything by just reading the text? It certainly is, provided that you concentrate your attention on the meaning and content of what you are reading. It is sufficient to know where *Aegyptus* is, to understand the statements *Aegyptus in Eurōpā nōn est, Aegyptus in Āfricā est* (l. 5). There can be no doubt about the meaning of *nōn* (a so-called negation). But often a sentence is understood only when seen together with other sentences. In the sentence *Hispānia quoque in Eurōpā est* (ll. 2-3) you will not understand *quoque* until you read in context: *Italia et Graecia in Eurōpā sunt. Hispānia quoque in Eurōpā est*. (The two preceding sentences might have been: *Italia in Eurōpā est. Graecia quoque in Eurōpā est*.) If you are still in doubt, just go on reading till the word recurs: *Syria nōn est in Eurōpā, sed in Asiā. Arabia quoque in Asiā est* (l. 7). Now you will certainly understand *quoque* – and in the meantime you have learned the word *sed* almost without noticing it.

the negation nōn
('......')

quoque ('........')

sed ('......')

In the next paragraph a number of questions are asked, and each question is followed by an answer. It is often necessary to read the answer before you can be quite sure of the meaning of the question. The first question is: *Estne Gallia in Eurōpā?* The *-ne* attached to *est* marks the sentence as a question (our question mark [?] was unknown to the ancient Romans). The answer is *Gallia in Eurōpā est*. The next question *Estne Rōma in Galliā?* is answered in the negative: *Rōma in Galliā nōn est*. (Latin has no single word for 'yes' or 'no', the sentence – or part of it – must be repeated with or without *nōn*).

-ne...? (question)

In the question *Ubi est Rōma?* the word *ubi* is intelligible only when you get the answer: *Rōma est in Italiā*.

After the short survey of the location of the principal Roman provinces, you are told about various localities: *Rhēnus* and *Nīlus*, *Corsica* and *Sardinia*, *Tūsculum* and *Brundisium*. You will find these names on the map, and the text will tell you what they represent. If you are still in doubt about the meaning of the words *fluvius*, *īnsula* and *oppidum*, turn back to the picture heading the chapter.

Note that these words occur in two different forms: *Nīlus* alone is called *fluvius*, but *Nīlus* and *Rhēnus* together are called *fluviī*. In similar circumstances you will notice the use of the forms *īnsula* and *īnsulae*, and *oppidum* and *oppida*. In the section GRAMMATICA LATINA you learn that the forms *fluvius*, *īnsula* and *oppidum* are called *singulāris*, while *fluviī*, *īnsulae* and *oppida* are called *plūrālis* – in English singular and plural.

As you read on you will see that *Nīlus* is referred to not only as *fluvius*, but as *fluvius magnus*, unlike *Tiberis*, which is described as *fluvius parvus*. In the same way *Sicilia* is referred to as *īnsula magna* as opposed to *Melita* (the modern Malta), which is called *īnsula parva*. In the margin *magnus* and *parvus* are represented as opposites (sign [↔], 'the opposite of'); this will help you to understand the meaning of the words, but note the changing endings. Further examples are seen when *Brundisium* is called *oppidum magnum* and *Tūsculum oppidum parvum*, and when the same words occur in the plural: *fluviī magnī*, *īnsulae magnae*, *oppida magna*.

A word which shows this variation between the endings *-us, -a, -um* in the singular and *-ī, -ae, -a* in the plural is called an adjective (Latin *adiectīvum*, 'added word') because it is added to a noun (substantive), which it qualifies. Other nouns occurring in this chapter are *prōvincia, imperium, numerus, littera, vocābulum*. Adjectives are, besides *magnus -a -um* and *parvus -a -um*, e.g. *Graecus -a -um*, *Rōmānus -a -um*, *Latīnus -a -um*, *prīmus -a -um*, and in the plural *multī -ae -a* and *paucī -ae -a*. The endings of the adjectives depend on the nouns that they qualify.

The question *Num Crēta oppidum est?* (l. 49) must of course be answered in the negative: *Crēta oppidum nōn est*. *Num* is an interrogative (i.e. asking) particle, like *-ne*, but a question beginning with *num* implies a negative answer. The next question is *Quid est Crēta?* Here, again, only the answer, *Crēta īnsula est*, makes the meaning of the question quite plain.

We have seen a final *-a* modified to *-ā* after *in*: *in Italiā, in Eurōpā, in Āfricā*. We now see that *in* also makes *-um* change to *-ō*: *in imperiō Rōmānō*; *in vocābulō*; *in capitulō prīmō* (ll. 58, 72, 73). These forms in *-ā* and *-ō* are dealt with in cap. 5.

As a numerical sign for 'a thousand', *mīlle*, the Romans took the Greek letter Φ (ph), which was rendered CIↃ and later changed into M under the influence of MILLE.

Latin is a concise language. It can often express in a few words what demands several words in other languages. One of the reasons is that Latin has fewer particles (small uninflected words) than most modern languages; thus you will find nothing corresponding to the English articles 'a' and 'the' as in 'a river', 'the river', etc.

Chapter 2

We now introduce you to the people whose daily lives you are going to read about. The picture shows them dressed in their best clothes, except for the four who are relegated to the margin – clearly they are not on the same level as the rest of the family. Be sure to remember the names, for you will soon become so well acquainted with these persons that you will almost feel like a friend visiting a real Roman family 2000 years ago. And the remarkable thing about it is that you can understand their language!

the Roman family

Note that the names of these people end in either *-us* or *-a*, none of them end in *-um*. You will see that the ending *-us* is characteristic of male persons *(Iūlius, Mārcus, Quīntus, Dāvus, Mēdus)* and *-a* of female persons *(Aemilia, Iūlia, Syra, Dēlia)*. This also applies to nouns that denote persons. Nouns referring to males generally end in *-us: filius, dominus, servus* (but *-us* is dropped in some nouns in *-r*, e.g. *vir, puer*), while nouns denoting females end mostly in *-a (fēmina, puella, filia, domina, ancilla);* but no persons are denoted by words ending in *-um.* We say therefore that nouns ending in *-um*, e.g. *oppidum, vocābulum, imperium,* are <u>neuter</u> (Latin *neutrum,* 'neither', i.e. neither masculine nor feminine), while most words in *-us* are <u>masculine</u> (Latin *masculīnum*), and most words in *-a* are <u>feminine</u> (Latin *fēminīnum,* from *fēmina*). But as grammatical terms 'masculine' and 'feminine' are not restricted to living beings: the words *fluvius, numerus, titulus, liber* are grammatically masculine, while *īnsula, littera, prōvincia, familia* are feminine. The grammatical term, therefore, is not 'sex', but <u>gender</u> (Latin *genus*). The abbreviations used for the three genders are *m, f* and *n.*

males: *-us*
females: *-a*

genders:
masculine (m.): *-us*
feminine (f.): *-a*
neuter (n.): *-um*

The word *familia* refers to the whole household, including all the slaves, *servī* and *ancillae,* who belong to the head of the family as his property. *Iūlius* is the father, *pater,* of *Mārcus, Quīntus* and *Iūlia,* and the master, *dominus,* of *Mēdus, Dāvus, Syra, Dēlia,* etc. To express these relationships we need the <u>genitive</u> (Latin *genetīvus*), a form of the noun ending in *-ī* or *-ae* in the singular: *Iūlius est pater Mārcī et Quīntī et Iūliae;* in the plural you find the long endings *-ōrum* and *-ārum: Iūlius est dominus multōrum servōrum et multārum ancillārum.* So the genitive endings are *-ae* and *-ārum* in the feminine, and *-ī* and *-ōrum* in the masculine – and in the neuter (see ll. 56, 87). In the section GRAMMATICA LATINA you find examples of all these forms. (English has the ending *-s* or 'of': 'Julia*'s* mother' or 'the mother *of* Julia'.)

genitive:
    m./n. f.
sing. *-ī*   *-ae*
plur. *-ōrum* *-ārum*

Particles like *et* and *sed* are called <u>conjunctions</u> (Latin *coniūnctiōnēs,* from *con-iungere,*'join') because they join words and sentences. Instead of *et* you often find the conjunction *-que* attached after the second word: *Dēlia Mēdus-que* stands for *Dēlia et Mēdus* and *filiī filiaeque* for *filiī et filiae* (ll. 9 and 22).

conjunctions

...*-que* = *et* ...

Among the new words in cap. 2 are the interrogative words *quis* and *quae,* which are used to ask questions about persons (English 'who'): *Quis est Mārcus?* and *Quae est Iūlia?* i.e. masculine *quis* (plural *quī*), feminine *quae* – and neuter *quid,* as you have seen in cap. 1 (English 'what'). The genitive of the interrogative for all genders is *cuius* (English 'whose'): *Cuius servus est Dāvus? Dāvus servus Iūliī est* (l. 35).

m.   f.   n.
quis? quae? quid?
gen. *cuius?*

The <u>invariable</u> interrogative particle *quot* asks questions about number: *Quot līberī sunt in familiā? In familiā Iūliī sunt trēs līberī. Quot filiī et quot filiae? Duo filiī et ūna filia. Quot servī...? ... centum servī* (ll. 37–39). Like most numerals *centum* is invariable; but *ūnus* has the familiar endings *-us -a -um,* the feminine of *duo* is *duae (duae filiae),* and the neuter of *trēs* is *tria (tria oppida).*

quot? 1, 2, 3...
m.   f.   n.
ūnus ūna ūnum
duo duae duo
trēs trēs tria

11

magnus numerus −ōrum
= multī −ī / multa −a
magnus numerus −ārum
= multae −ae

The number can also be indicated by the noun *numerus* combined with the genitive plural: *Numerus līberōrum est trēs. Numerus servōrum est centum* (ll. 43-44). As *centum* must be said to be *magnus numerus,* the following sentences are easily understood: *Numerus servōrum est magnus* and *In familiā magnus numerus servōrum est.* It appears that *magnus numerus servōrum* is equivalent to *multī servī.* In the same way *parvus numerus līberōrum* has the same meaning as *paucī līberī.* Besides you will find the expressions *magnus numerus oppidōrum* and *fluviōrum* meaning *multa oppida* and *multī fluviī.*

cēterī -ae -a

The Romans only knew the northern part of the continent of Africa, where there is only one big river, the Nile: *In Āfricā ūnus fluvius magnus est: Nīlus* (l. 58). It goes on: *Cēterī fluviī Āfricae parvī sunt.* The adjective *cēterī -ae -a*, 'the other(s)', recurs several times, thus the enumeration of the first three of the 35 *capitula* (l. 86) is concluded with *cētera* (it might have been *et cētera,* the Latin expression which gives us the abbreviation 'etc.').

enumeration:
(1) *A et B et C*
(2) *A, B, C*
(3) *A, B C-que*

The following rule applies to enumerations in Latin: (1) *et* put between all items: *Mārcus et Quīntus et Iūlia;* or (2) no conjunction used at all: *Mārcus, Quīntus, Iūlia;* or (3) *-que* added to the last item: *Mārcus, Quīntus Iūliaque.*

meus -a -um
tuus -a -um

The conversation at the end of the chapter shows that instead of the genitive the adjectives *meus -a -um* and *tuus -a -um* are used to refer to what belongs to the person speaking or the person spoken to respectively (like English 'my' and 'your').

ecce: ⟶

On page 16 you come across the word *ecce* (illustrated with an arrow in the margin). It is used when you point to or call attention to something, in this case to the picture of the two books. Notice the form of an ancient book: a scroll with the text written in columns, and the Latin word for such a scroll: *liber* (another masculine noun in *-er* without *-us*), plural *librī.*

sing. plur.
liber librī

Chapter 3

Now that you have been introduced to the family, you are going to watch some of their doings. We begin with the children – they were very much the same in ancient times as they are today. So we are not surprised to learn that Julius and Aemilia's children cannot always get on together. Here little Julia is the first to suffer, because she is annoying her big brother. Peace is not restored until Mother and Father step in.

verbs:
-at: cantat, pulsat, plōrat
-et: rīdet, videt, respondet
-it: venit, audit, dormit

Several of the new words in this chapter are verbs. A verb (Latin *verbum*) is a word that expresses an action or a state: that someone does something or that something exists or takes place. The first Latin verb you come across is *cantat* in the opening sentence: *Iūlia cantat.* Other verbs are *pulsat, plōrat, rīdet, videt, vocat, venit,* etc. They all end in *-t* – like *est,* which is also a verb – and mostly come at the end of the sentence.

The first of the two words in the sentence *Iūlia cantat* denotes the person who performs the action. Other sentences of the same kind are: *Iūlia plōrat; Mārcus rīdet; Aemilia venit; pater dormit* (ll. 9, 10, 21, 37). But it is not always as simple as this. Take for instance the sentence that is illustrated by the little drawing in the margin: *Mārcus Iūliam pulsat* (l. 8). Here we are told not only who performs the action, but also who the action is aimed at. The same pattern is seen in the following sentences, also illustrated by pictures: *Quīntus Mārcum videt; Quīntus Mārcum pulsat; Mārcus Quīntum pulsat; Iūlia Aemiliam vocat.*

Mārcus Iūliam pulsat

Quīntus Mārcum videt
Iūlia Aemiliam vocat

12

As you see, the name of the person who performs the action, the so-called <u>subject</u> of the verb, has one of the well-known endings *-us* and *-a,* whereas the name of the person toward whom the action is directed, the <u>object</u>, takes the ending *-um* or *-am.* In other words: *Iūlia* is changed to *Iūliam* when we are told that Marcus hits her, just as *Mārcus* becomes *Mārcum* when he is the victim. In similar circumstances *puella* changes to *puellam,* and *puer* to *puerum,* and qualifying adjectives get the same ending: *Mārcus parvam puellam pulsat; Iūlius puerum improbum verberat.*

Thus with the help of the endings we distinguish in Latin between the <u>subject</u> and the <u>object</u> of the verb. The forms in *-us* and *-a,* which characterize the subject, are called <u>nominative</u> (Latin *nōminātīvus*), and the forms in *-um* and *-am,* which denote the object, are called <u>accusative</u> (Latin *accūsātīvus*). Verbs like *pulsat, videt, vocat,* which are used with an object in the accusative, are called <u>transitive</u>, and verbs without an object, e.g. *plōrat, venit, dormit,* are <u>intransitive</u> verbs.

subject object verb
Mārcus Iūliam pulsat
  m.   f.
nominative: *-us* *-a*
accusative: *-um -am*

transitive & intransitive verbs

Instead of accusatives in *-am* and *-um* you sometimes find *eam* and *eum,* e.g. *Iūlia plōrat quia Mārcus eam pulsat* and *Cūr Iūlius Quīntum nōn audit? Iūlius eum nōn audit, quia dormit* (ll. 27, 43; the colon in the marginal note *eam : Iūliam* means that <u>here</u> *eam* stands for *Iūliam*). A word of this kind, which takes the place of a name or noun, is called a <u>pronoun</u> (Latin *prōnōmen,* from *prō* 'instead of' and *nōmen* 'name' or 'noun'). Corresponding to *eum* and *eam* the pronoun *mē* is used when a person is speaking about him- or herself, and *tē* is used about the person spoken to (in English 'me' and 'you'): *Aemilia: "Quis mē vocat?" Quīntus: "Iūlia tē vocat"* (ll. 24-25).

eam : Iūliam
eum : Quīntum

pronoun
  m.   f.
acc. *eum eam*
      mē
      tē

The interrogative particle *cūr* is used to ask about the cause (Latin *causa*). A question introduced by *cūr* calls for an answer with the <u>causal conjunction</u> *quia* (English 'because'): *Cūr Iūlia plōrat? Iūlia plōrat, quia Mārcus eam pulsat. Cūr Mārcus Iūliam pulsat? Quia Iūlia cantat* (ll. 26-27, 30-31).

question: *cūr ...?*
answer: *... quia ...*

When the identity of the subject is known, because the context shows who it is, it need not be repeated (or replaced by a pronoun) in a following sentence: *"Ubi est Iūlius? Cūr nōn venit?"* (l. 36); *Iūlius eum nōn audit, quia dormit* (l. 43); *"Cūr māter Mārcum verberat?" "Mārcum verberat, quia puer improbus est"* (l. 58). (In English we use the pronouns 'he' and 'she'.)

subject implied

The conjunctions *et* and *sed* are not combined with a negation; instead of *et nōn* and *sed nōn* the conjunction *neque (ne-que)* is used, i.e. *-que* attached to the original negation *ne* (= *nōn*): *Iūlius dormit neque Quīntum audit. Iūlius venit, neque Aemilia eum videt* (in English 'and not', 'but not').

ne-que = et nōn (sed nōn)

In the sentence *Puer quī parvam puellam pulsat improbus est* (l. 63) *quī* is the <u>relative</u> pronoun, which refers to *puer.* At the end of the chapter (p. 23) you find sentences with both the <u>interrogative</u> and the relative pronoun, e. g. *Quis est puer quī rīdet?* In the feminine the two pronouns are identical: *Quae est puella quae plōrat?* (the relative *quae* refers to *puella*). The interrogative pronoun *quis* is *quem* in the accusative: *Quem vocat Quīntus? Quīntus Iūlium vocat.* As a relative pronoun *quem* is used in the masculine and *quam* in the feminine: *Puer quem Aemilia verberat est Mārcus. Puella quam Mārcus pulsat est Iūlia.* The examples show that *quī* and *quem* (m.) refer to a masculine noun, and *quae* and *quam* (f.) to a feminine noun. In cap. 4 (l. 75) you will meet *quod,* which refers to a neuter noun: *baculum, quod in mēnsā est.*

relative pronoun
puer quī ...
puella quae...
interrogative pronoun
nom. *quis*
acc. *quem*

relative pronoun
  m.   f.   n.
nom. *quī quae quod*
acc. *quem quam quod*

13

Chapter 4

We now leave the children for a while and turn to the grown-ups. There is a worried look on Julius's face; it turns out that a sum of money is missing. Who is the thief? The problem is not solved until the end of the chapter, of course – and by then the culprit has already decamped! Later (in cap. 6 and 8) you will find out where he is hiding and what he does with the money. But right now you must set to work to discover who is the thief.

In addressing a man in Latin the nominative in -us is replaced by a special form, the vocative (Latin *vocātīvus,* from *vocat*), ending in -e. Medus calls Davus crying: *"Dāve!"* (l. 25) and when Davus greets his master he says: *"Salvē, domine!"* and Julius answers: *"Salvē, serve!"* (ll. 34-35).

The form of the verb used to give orders is called the imperative (Latin *imperātīvus,* from *imperat*). The Latin imperative consists of the shortest form of the verb, without any ending, the so-called stem, e.g. *vocā! tacē! venī!* or a short -e is added when the stem ends in a consonant, as in *pōne!* (the stem is *pōn-*). Examples: ll. 24, 27, 37, 60, etc.

The stem of a Latin verb ends in one of the long vowels -ā, -ē, -ī, or in a consonant. The verbs are therefore divided into four classes, so-called conjugations:

1st conjugation: ā-verbs, with stems ending in -ā: *vocā-, cantā-, pulsā-.*
2nd conjugation: ē-verbs, with stems ending in -ē: *tacē-, vidē-, habē-.*
3rd conjugation: consonant-verbs, with stems ending in a consonant: *pōn-, sūm-, discēd-.*
4th conjugation: ī-verbs, with stems ending in -ī: *venī-, audī-, dormī-.*

To these stems the different verbal endings are added (a vertical stroke [|] is here used to mark the division between stem and ending). When -t is added the last vowel of the stem becomes short: *voca|t, vide|t, veni|t,* and in the consonant-verbs a short -i- is inserted before the -t: *pōn|it, sūm|it, discēd|it.* This verbal form is called the indicative (Latin *indicātīvus,* 'stating', 'declaring').

In the second of the two sentences *Mēdus discēdit, quia is pecūniam dominī habet* (l. 77) the nominative *Mēdus* is replaced by the pronoun *is,* which is the nominative corresponding to the accusative *eum* (English 'he' and 'him'). But the nominative of this pronoun is only used when it carries a certain emphasis (here Medus is contrasted with Davus). When the subject is not emphasized, the verb is used with no pronoun, e.g. *Mēdus nōn respondet, quia abest* (l. 85; in English we cannot do without the pronoun.)

The genitive of *is* is *eius* (cf. English 'his'): *In sacculō eius (: Iūliī) est pecūnia* (l. 1). However, referring to something that belongs to the subject of the sentence, the adjective *suus -a -um* is used instead of *eius.* Compare the two examples: *Dāvus sacculum suum in mēnsā pōnit* and *Iam sacculus eius in mēnsā est* (ll. 61-62). (In English the word 'own' is sometimes added to make the meaning plain: 'his/ her own').

After *in* not only -um but also -us becomes -ō: *Sacculus Iūliī nōn parvus est. In sacculō eius est pecūnia* (l. 3). This form will be treated in cap. 5.

The adjectives *meus -a -um, tuus -a -um* and *suus -a -um* are called possessive pronouns. The possesive pronouns serve to replace the genitive.

14

Chapter 5

We have made the acquaintance of what is evidently a prosperous Roman family, to judge from the splendid villa in which they live. The plan on page 33 and the pictures of various parts of the house will give you an impression of the layout of this typical Roman villa. Characteristic features are the atrium with its opening in the roof and pool for rainwater, and the peristyle, the inner courtyard lined with rows of columns.

the Roman villa

The first new grammatical point to be learned is the <u>accusative plural</u>. Corresponding to the accusative singular in -*um* and -*am*, which was introduced in cap. 3, you now find plural forms ending in -*ōs* and -*ās* respectively: the plural *fīliī* becomes *fīliōs* when it is the object of the verb: *Iūlius duōs fīliōs habet;* similarly *fīliae* changes to *fīliās* (see ll. 3-4). The accusative of masculine and feminine nouns always ends in -*m* in the singular and in -*s* in the plural. Neuter nouns have the same ending in the accusative as in the nominative (sing. -*um*, plur. -*a*).

<u>accusative</u> sing. & plur.

	m.	f.	n.
sing.	-um	-am	-um
plur.	-ōs	-ās	-a

Secondly, you will see that the particles *ab, cum, ex, in* and *sine* cause the following nouns to take the ending -*ō* (m./n.) or -*ā* (f.) in the plural -*īs*: *ex hortō, ab Aemiliā, in ātriō, cum līberīs, sine rosīs.* Such prefixed words are called <u>prepositions</u> (Latin *praepositiōnēs*, 'placing in front'). You have already seen examples of the preposition *in: in Italiā, in imperiō Rōmānō, in sacculō.* The forms in -*ō*, -*ā* and -*īs* are called <u>ablative</u> (Latin *ablātīvus*). The prepositions *ab, cum, ex, in, sine* are said to 'take' the ablative.

<u>prepositions</u>
ab, cum, ex, in, sine
+ -*ō*/-*ā*/-*īs*

<u>ablative</u>

	m./n.	f.
sing.	-ō	-ā
plur.	-īs	

New forms of the pronoun *is* are now introduced: feminine *ea*, neuter *id*; plural *iī* (= *eī*), *eae*, *ea*. In the accusative and ablative this pronoun shows the same endings as the noun it represents; remembering the accusatives *eum* and *eam* you will identify forms like *eō*, *eā* (abl. sing.), *eōs*, *eās* (acc. plur.) and *iīs* (= *eīs*, abl. plur.). The genitive plural is *eōrum*, *eārum* (thus for *dominus servōrum* you find *dominus eōrum*), but the genitive singular has a special form *eius*, which is the same for all three genders: you have already had *sacculus eius* (: *Iūliī*), now you find *nāsus eius* (: *Syrae*, l. 18). (These genitives correspond to the English possessive pronouns 'his/her/its/their'.)

<u>pronoun</u> *is ea id*

sing.	m.	f.	n.
nom.	is	ea	id
acc.	eum	eam	id
gen.	eius	eius	eius
abl.	eō	eā	eō
plur.			
nom.	iī	eae	ea
acc.	eōs	eās	ea
gen.	eōrum	eārum	eōrum
abl.	iīs	iīs	iīs

Lastly, you learn plural forms of verbs: (1) when the subject is in the plural or more than one person, the verb ends, not in -*t* only, but in -*nt* (cf. *est* and *sunt*): *Mārcus et Quīntus Iūliam vocant. Puerī rīdent;* and (2) when two or more people are ordered to do something, the plural form of the imperative ending in -*te* is used: *Mārce et Quīnte! Iūliam vocāte! Tacēte, puerī! Audīte!* In the consonant-verbs (3rd conjugation) a short vowel is inserted before these plural endings: -*i*- before -*te* and -*u*- before -*nt*: *Discēdite, puerī! Puerī discēdunt.* Even in the *ī*-verbs (4th conjugation) -*u*- is inserted before -*nt*: *Puerī veniunt.*

<u>imperative & indicative</u>

	sing.	plur.
1. imp.	vocā	vocā|te
ind.	voca|t	voca|nt
2. imp.	vidē	vidē|te
ind.	vide|t	vide|nt
3. imp.	pōn|e	pōn|ite
ind.	pōn|it	pōn|unt
4. imp.	audī	audī|te
ind.	audi|t	audi|unt

Julia's remark *"puerī mē rīdent"* (l. 70) shows that *rīdet*, which is usually an intransitive verb, can take an object in the sense 'laugh at': *puerī Iūliam rīdent.*

rīdet + acc.

The consonant-verb *agit agunt* denotes action in general: *Quid agit Mārcus? Quid agunt puerī?* (English 'do'). The imperative of this verb is often put before another imperative to emphasize the command, e.g. *Age! venī, serve! Agite! venīte, servī!*

age! agite! + imp.

15

Chapter 6

Road communications were highly developed in the ancient Roman world. The different parts of the Roman Empire were connected by an excellent network of highways. On the map on page 40 you see the most important Roman roads in Italy, among them the famous Via Appia, running southward from Rome and continuing all the way to Brundisium.

Running almost parallel to the Via Appia is the Via Latina, which passes the town of Tusculum mentioned in the first chapter. Julius's villa stands in the neighborhood of this town, so that anyone going from there to Rome must follow the Via Latina. Therefore it is not surprising to find Medus walking along this road. You will soon discover what it is that attracts him to the city.

prep. + acc.:
ad, ante, apud, circum,
inter, per, post, prope

In cap. 5 you met some common prepositions that take the ablative. Most other prepositions take the accusative, e.g. *ad, ante, apud, circum, inter, per, post, prope*, which are now introduced. *Ad* indicates motion to a place – it is the opposite of *ab* (followed by the ablative!) which indicates motion away from a place. The corresponding interrogative particles are *quō* and *unde: Quō it Iūlius? Ad vīllam it. Unde venit? Ab oppidō.* – Instead of *ab* we often find the shortened form *ā* before a consonant, but never before a vowel or *h-: ā vīllā, ā dominō, ab ancillā, ab oppidō.*

quō? ad + acc.
unde? ab + abl.

ab + vowel & *h-*
ā/ab + cons. (except *h-*)

quō? Tūsculum
Rōmam
unde? Tūsculō
Rōmā

Motion to or from a town mentioned by name is expressed by the name of the town in the accusative or ablative respectively without a preposition. In Latin therefore we speak of traveling *Rōmā–Brundisium*, or, if going in the opposite direction, *Brundisiō–Rōmam.* It is the fundamental function of the ablative (with or without a preposition) to denote 'place from which'. In this function it is called ablative of separation (*ablātīvus* means 'taking away').

ablative of separation

To indicate where something or somebody is, the preposition *in* followed by the ablative is most often used: *in Italiā, in oppidō, in hortō.* The examples *Cornēlius Tūsculī habitat* and *Mēdus Rōmae est* show, however, that *in* is no more used with names of towns than *ad* and *ab;* instead the name takes the ending *-ī* or *-ae* according as the nominative ends in *-um/-us* or *-a.* This form, which here coincides with the genitive, is called locative (Latin *locātīvus,* from *locus,* 'place'). Examples: ll. 47, 59, 77, 85.

ubi? Tūsculī
Rōmae

locative (= genitive)
-ī, -ae

Mārcus Iūliam pulsat =
Iūlia pulsātur ā Mārcō

The Latin sentence *Mārcus Iūliam pulsat* can be turned into *Iūlia pulsātur ā Mārcō* (as in English 'Marcus hits Julia' and 'Julia is hit by Marcus'). The action is the same, but in the second sentence, where the verb ends in *-tur,* the active person, who performs the action, steps into the background, while the passive person, the 'sufferer', comes to the front: she appears no longer as object in the accusative *(Iūliam),* but as subject in the nominative *(Iūlia),* and the name of the person by whom the action is performed, the agent, is in the ablative preceded by *ab* or *ā (ā Mārcō).* On page 44 you find several examples of the two constructions, which are called active and passive respectively (Latin *āctīvum* and *passīvum*). In the sentence *Mēdus Lȳdiam amat et ab eā amātur* (ll. 78-79) the two constructions are combined.

active	passive
1. *voca|t*	*vocā|tur*
voca|nt	*voca|ntur*
2. *vide|t*	*vidē|tur*
vide|nt	*vide|ntur*
3. *pōn|it*	*pōn|itur*
pōn|unt	*pōn|untur*
4. *audi|t*	*audī|tur*
audi|unt	*audi|untur*

In the passive, as we have seen, the personal agent is expressed by *ab/ā* and the ablative. When no person is involved, the ablative is used without *ab/ā,* e.g. *Cornēlius equō vehitur; Lȳdia verbīs Mēdī dēlectātur.* The simple ablative here indicates means or cause. This is very common both in passive and active sentences: *Iūlius lectīcā vehitur. Dominus servum baculō verberat. Servī saccōs umerīs portant. Mēdus viā Latīnā Rōmam ambulat.* This use of the ablative is called ablative of instrument (Latin *ablātīvus īnstrūmentī*) or ablative of means.

Cornēlius equō vehitur =
equus Cornēlium vehit

ablative of instrument or
ablative of means

16

Chapter 7

When Father comes back from town, he usually brings something with him for the family. So in this chapter you find out what there is in the two sacks that Syrus and Leander have been carrying.

When we are told that Julius gives something to a member of the family, the name of this person ends in *-ō (Mārcō, Quīntō, Syrō, Lēandrō)* or in *-ae (Aemiliae, Iūliae, Syrae, Dēliae)*. This form, ending in *-ō* in the masculine (and neuter) and in *-ae* in the feminine, is called <u>dative</u> (Latin *datīvus*, from *dat*, 'gives'). Examples: *Iūlius Mārcō/fīliō suō mālum dat* (ll. 45-47); *Iūlius Aemiliae ōsculum dat* (l. 63). Instead of *Iūlius Syrō et Lēandrō māla dat* we find *Iūlius servīs māla dat*, and in the sentence *Iūlius ancillīs māla dat* Syra and Delia are referred to. In the plural the dative ends in *-īs* like the ablative.

<u>dative</u>
	m./n.	f.
sing.	-ō	-ae
plur.	-īs	

The dative of the pronoun *is ea id* is *eī* in the singular and *iīs* (or *eīs*) in the plural: *Iūlius eī (: Quīntō/Iūliae) mālum dat. Iūlius iīs (: servīs/ancillīs) māla dat*. The forms are the same for all three genders. The dative (sing.) of the interrogative and relative pronoun is *cui: Cui Iūlius mālum dat? Puer/puella cui Iūlius mālum dat est fīlius/fīlia eius* (see ll. 101-104).

pronoun *is ea id*
dative: sing. *eī*, plur. *iīs*

interrog. & rel. pronoun
dative sing. *cui*

The examples *Puella sē in speculō videt et sē interrogat* (ll. 8-9) show that the pronoun *sē* (acc.) is used when referring to the subject in the same sentence; *sē* is called the <u>reflexive</u> pronoun (English 'himself/herself/themselves').

the <u>reflexive</u> pronoun
sē (acc.)

Compare the sentences *Iūlius in vīllā est* and *Iūlius in vīllam intrat*. In the first sentece *in* takes the ablative *(vīllā)*, as we have seen so often; in the second it is followed by the accusative *(vīllam)*. The examples show that *in* takes the accusative when there is motion <u>into</u> a place. Therefore we read: *Syra in cubiculum intrat*, and she says: *"Venī in hortum, Iūlia!"* (ll. 14, 17).

in + abl./acc.
ubi? in vīllā
quō? in vīllam

A question introduced with *num* calls for a negative answer; therefore Julia asks: *"Num nāsus meus foedus est?"* (l. 20). The opposite effect is obtained by *nōnne:* when Syra asks *"Nōnne fōrmōsus est nāsus meus?"* (l. 26) she certainly expects the answer to be 'yes'. Nevertheless Julia says: *"Immō foedus est!"* The word *immō* serves to stress a denial (English 'no', 'on the contrary').

question: answer:
nōnne... est? ..t. est
num... est? ... nōn est

The imperative of *est* is *es!* (i.e. the stem without an ending; plural *este!*): *"Tergē oculōs! Es laeta!"* (l. 23). – The greeting *Salvē!* expresses a wish for good health. It was understood as an imperative, so it has a plural form in *-te: "Salvēte, fīliī!"* (l. 31).

es|t: imp. *es! es|te!*

sing. *salvē!*
plur. *salvē|te!*

Note the repetition of the conjunctions *et* and *neque* (ll. 50, 57): *et Mārcus et Quīntus māla habent* and *Servī neque māla neque pira habent* (English 'both ... and' and 'neither... nor'). Instead of *et... et* we often find *nōn sōlum... sed etiam: nōn sōlum māla, sed etiam pira* (l. 56).

et... et
neque... neque

nōn sōlum... sed etiam

Referring to things close to him, Julius says e.g. *hic saccus* and *hoc mālum*, and Julia says *haec rosa* of the rose that she is holding (ll. 43, 90, 85). The <u>demonstrative</u> pronoun *hic haec hoc* (English 'this') is treated in cap. 8. – *Hic saccus plēnus mālōrum est* (l. 43): note the <u>genitive</u> after *plēnus* ('full of...').

hic haec hoc

plēnus + gen.

<u>Compound</u> verbs have often prepositions as their first element, like *ad-est* and *ab-est*. In this chapter you find *in-est, ad-venit, ad-it, ex-it*, in the next *ab-it*. Often the same preposition is put before a noun in the same sentence: *Quid inest in saccīs? Iūlius ad vīllam advenit. Iūlia ē cubiculō exit*.

<u>compounds</u> with prepositions:
ad-, ab-, ex-, in-

The last example shows the shorter form *ē* of the preposition *ex*. The same rule applies to the use of *ex* and *ē* as to *ab* and *ā:* before vowels and *h-* only *ex* and *ab* are used; *ē* and *ā* are only used before consonants, never before vowels or *h-*. Examples with *ex* and *ē: ē/ex vīllā*, but only *ex ātriō, ex hortō*.

ex + vowel & *h-*
ē/ex + cons. (except *h-*)

17

Chapter 8

In the ancient world people did their shopping over open counters lining the streets. Passers-by could simply stand on the sidewalk in front of a shop and buy what they wanted. We can be sure that the shopkeepers, with Mediterranean eloquence, gave their customers every encouragement.

In this chapter we pay particular attention to some important underlined pronouns: the interrogative pronoun *quis quae quid*, the relative pronoun *quī quae quod*, and the demonstrative pronouns *is ea id, hic haec hoc* and *ille illa illud*. Of the last two *hic haec hoc* refers to something that is here *(hīc)*, i.e. near the speaker, while *ille illa illud* refers to something that is further away from the speaker (English 'this' and 'that'). These demonstrative pronouns are mostly used as adjectives qualifying nouns: *hic vir, haec fēmina, hoc oppidum* and *ille vir, illa fēmina, illud oppidum*. Of *hic haec hoc* the invariable stem is just *h-*, cf. the plural *hī hae, hōs hās, hōrum hārum, hīs*, but in the singular (and in the neuter plural nom./acc.) a *-c* is added (see the survey on p. 61).

The forms of the other pronouns are shown in systematically arranged examples in the section GRAMMATICA LATINA. Here not only *ille -a -ud*, but also *is ea id* is used as an adjective: *is servus, ea ancilla, id ōrnāmentum* (English 'that'). The interrogative pronoun is also used before nouns as an adjective: *quī servus? quae ancilla? quod oppidum?* Note that in the masculine and neuter the adjectival forms used before nouns are *quī* and *quod* respectively, while *quis* and *quid* are used alone (however, *quis* is also used before a noun in questions of identity: *quis servus? Mēdus*). – When the relative pronoun is used without an antecedent to refer to, as in *Quī tabernam habet, tabernārius est* and *Quī magnam pecūniam habent ōrnāmenta emunt* (ll. 3, 16), a demonstrative pronoun may be understood: *is quī..., iī quī...* (cf. ll. 14, 35, 101)

Like *ille -a -ud* most pronouns have the endings *-īus* in the genitive and *-ī* in the dative in all three genders (but the *i* is short or consonantal in *eius, cuius, huius, cui, huic*). The neuter ending *-ud* is also found in *alius -a -ud* (l. 33).

The verbs *accipit* and *aspicit* have plural forms in *-iunt: accipiunt, aspiciunt*, and imperatives in *-e -ite: accipe! accipite!* and *aspice! aspicite!* They seem to follow a pattern which is neither that of the consonant-verbs nor that of the *ī*-verbs. This is because the stem of these verbs ends in a short *i: accipi-, aspici-;* but this *i* appears only before an ending beginning with a vowel, such as *-unt: accipiunt, aspiciunt;* otherwise these verbs behave like consonant-verbs and are regarded as belonging to the 3rd conjugation.

Instead of *tam magnus* and *quam magnus* the adjectives *tantus* and *quantus* (ll. 64, 72) are used, and *tantus quantus* stands for *tam magnus quam: Pretium illīus ānulī tantum est quantum huius* (l. 75). – *Quam* is used in exclamations: *"Ō, quam pulchra sunt illa ōrnāmenta!"* (l. 42).

Note the ablative of instrument (without prepositions): *fēminae ōrnāmentīs dēlectantur* (l. 12); *gemmīs et margarītīs ānulīsque ōrnantur* (l. 24); *Lȳdia tabernam Albīnī digitō mōnstrat* (l. 43, i.e. 'points to'). With the verbs *emit, vēndit* and *cōnstat* (verbs of buying and selling, etc.) the price is in the ablative, so-called *ablātīvus pretiī* ('ablative of price'). Examples: *Hic ānulus centum nummīs cōnstat* (l. 59); *Albīnus... Mēdō ānulum vēndit sēstertiīs nōnāgintā* (ll. 116-117).

In the last example *Mēdō* is dative with *vēndit*. The dative now occurs also with *ostendit* (ll. 46, 52, 58, 83) and *mōnstrat* (l. 130). Being transitive these verbs have an object in the accusative, which is often called the direct object to distinguish it from the dative, which is called the indirect object.

18

Chapter 9

By studying the landscape above the chapter you will learn a great many new Latin nouns. In the words *campus, herba, rīvus, umbra, silva, caelum* you see the familiar endings *-us, -a, -um;* but the remaining words, *collis, pāstor, canis, mōns, sōl*, etc., have quite different endings, not only in the nominative, but also in the other <u>cases</u> (acc., gen., dat., abl.): in the singular they have the ending *-em* in the accusative, *-is* in the genitive, *-ī* in the dative, and *-e* in the ablative; in the plural they have *-ēs* in the nominative and accusative, *-um* or *-ium* in the genitive, and *-ibus* in the dative and ablative. Examples of all these endings are shown with the nouns *ovis* and *pāstor* (ll. 3–7, 11–18). Words <u>declined</u> (i.e. inflected) in this way are said to belong to the <u>3rd declension</u> (Latin *dēclīnātiō tertia*), whereas the <u>1st declension</u> *(dēclīnātiō prīma)* comprises words in *-a*, like *fēmina,* and the <u>2nd declension</u> *(dēclīnātiō secunda)* words in *-us (-er)* and *-um*, like *servus (liber)* and *oppidum*.

In the nominative singular 3rd declension nouns have either no ending (e.g. *pāstor, sōl, arbor*) or *-is* (e.g. *ovis, canis, pānis, collis*), *-ēs* (e.g. *nūbēs*), or just *-s:* this *-s* causes changes in the stem, e.g. the loss of *t* in *mōns* and *dēns* < *mont|s, dent|s,* gen. *mont|is, dent|is.* The nouns with no ending in the nominative are <u>consonant-stems</u>, the nouns in *-is* (or *-s*) were originally <u>*i*-stems</u>, but the endings have come to agree with the consonant-stems (only in the genitive plural in *-ium* the *i* appears clearly).

The 3rd declension nouns in this chapter are masculine or feminine, but the endings being the same for the two genders you cannot determine the gender of such nouns until they are combined with adjectives of the 1st and 2nd declensions (like *magnus -a -um*): the combinations *pāstor fessus, parvus collis, magnus mōns* and *ovis alba, magna vallis, multae arborēs* show that *pāstor, collis* and *mōns* are masculine and that *ovis, vallis* and *arbor* are feminine. In the margin and in the vocabulary gender is indicated by *m, f* and *n*.

In the GRAMMATICA LATINA section you will find examples of these three declensions. Take advantage of this opportunity to review the case-forms of *īnsula* (1st declension), *servus* and *verbum* (2nd declension), and then study the new 3rd declension (examples: *pāstor* and *ovis*).

The verb in the sentence *Ovēs herbam <u>edunt</u>* (l. 9) is a consonant-verb, as shown by the plural ending *-unt;* but the singular is irregular: *Pāstor pānem <u>ēst</u>* (only in Late Latin does the "regular" form *edit* appear). Also note the short imperative *dūc!* (l. 65, without *-e*) of the consonant-verb *dūc|it dūc|unt.*

The <u>temporal conjunction</u> *dum* expresses simultaneousness (English 'while'): *<u>Dum</u> pāstor in herbā dormit, ovis nigra... abit* (l. 39). After *exspectat* it comes to mean 'until': *Ovis cōnsistit et exspectat <u>dum</u> lupus venit* (l. 69).

New prepositions are *suprā*, which takes the accusative, and *sub*, which takes the ablative (when motion is implied *sub* takes the accusative).

The demonstrative pronoun *ipse* is used for emphasis like English 'himself /herself/itself': *Ubi est lupus <u>ipse</u>?* (l. 55). It is declined like *ille* apart from the neuter in *-um* (not *-ud*): *ipse -a -um.*

When *ad* and *in* enter into compounds with *currit* and *pōnit* they change to *ac-* and *im-*: *a<u>c</u>-currit, i<u>m</u>-pōnit.* Such a change, which makes one consonant like or similar to another (*m* is a labial consonant like *p*), is called <u>assimilation</u> (from Latin *similis*, 'similar', 'like').

<u>cases</u>:
nom., acc., gen., dat., abl.

<u>1st declension</u>
nom. *-a*, gen. *-ae*
<u>2nd declension</u>
nom. *-us/-um*, gen. *-ī*
<u>3rd declension</u>

	sing.	plur.
nom.	*-/-(i)s*	*-ēs*
acc.	*-em*	*-ēs*
gen.	*-is*	*-(i)um*
dat.	*-ī*	*-ibus*
abl.	*-e*	*-ibus*

consonant-stems:
gen. plur. *-um*
i-stems:
gen. plur. *-ium*

sing. *ēst*
plur. *edunt*

dūcit:
imp. *dūc! dūc|ite!*

suprā + acc.
sub + abl. (acc.)

ipse -a -um

<u>assimilation</u>:
a<u>d</u>-c... > *a<u>c</u>-c...*
i<u>n</u>-p... > *i<u>m</u>-p...*

19

Chapter 10

3rd declension m./f.
leō leōn|is m.
homō homin|is m.
vōx vōc|is f.
pēs ped|is m.

nēmō < *nē* + *homō*

3rd declension n.
flūmen flūmin|is
mar|e mar|is
animal animāl|is

conjunctions:
cum, temporal
quod, causal (= *quia*)

sing. *pot-est*
plur. *pos-sunt*

infinitive: *-re*

infinitive	
active	passive
vocā|re	*vocā|rī*
vidē|re	*vidē|rī*
pōn|ere	*pōn|ī*
audī|re	*audī|rī*

sing. *vult*
plur. *volunt*

impersonal:
necesse est (+ dat.)

amāre (< *amā|se*)

infinitive *-se:*
es|se
ēs|se (< *ed|se*)

ablātīvus modī

In this chapter several new 3rd declension nouns are introduced. Some of them have peculiar forms in the nominative singular: in *leō* an *-n* is dropped: gen. *leōn|is*. In *homō* this is combined with a vowel change: gen. *homin|is*. The *-s* ending produces the spelling *-x* for *-cs* in *vōx:* gen. *vōc|is*, and the loss of *d* in *pēs:* gen. *ped|is*. From now on the nominative and genitive of new nouns will be found in the margin. – *Homō* combined with the negation *nē* forms the pronoun *nēmō* (< *nē* + *homō,* 'nobody').

You also meet the first <u>neuter</u> nouns of the 3rd declension: *flūmen, mare, animal,* which in the plural (nom./acc.) end in *-a: flūmina, maria, animālia.* The declension of these nouns will be taken up in the next chapter

In <u>*Cum*</u> *avis volat, ālae moventur* (l. 15) *cum* is a <u>temporal</u> conjunction (English 'when'; cf. ll. 16, 51, 87). And in *Hominēs ambulāre possunt, quod pedēs habent* (l. 24) *quod* is a <u>causal</u> conjunction (= *quia;* cf. ll. 90, 128).

The verb *potest,* which first appears in the sentence *Canis volāre nōn <u>potest</u>* (l. 21), denotes ability (English 'is able to', 'can'). It is a compound with *est: pot-est;* the first element *pot-* (meaning 'able') is changed before *s* by assimilation to *pos-: Hominēs ambulāre po<u>s</u>-sunt* (l. 23).

Vol<u>āre</u> and *ambul<u>āre</u>* are the first examples of the basic verb form which is called the <u>infinitive</u> (Latin *īnfīnītīvus*) and ends in *-re.* In *ā-, ē-* and *ī-*verbs (1st, 2nd and 4th conjugations) this ending is added directly to the stem: *volā|re, vidē|re, audī|re.* In consonant-verbs (3rd conjugation) a short *e* is inserted before the ending: *pōn|<u>e</u>re.* From now on the infinitive will be the form of new verbs shown in the margin, so that you can always tell which of the four conjugations the verb belongs to: 1. *-āre;* 2. *-ēre;* 3. *-ere;* 4. *-īre.*

The sentence *Hominēs deōs vidē<u>re</u> nōn possunt* becomes in the passive: *Deī ab hominibus vidē<u>rī</u> nōn possunt. Vidērī* is the <u>passive infinitive</u> corresponding to the active *vidēre.* In the passive, *ā-, ē-* and *ī-*verbs have the ending *-rī* in the infinitive, e.g. *vidē|<u>rī</u>, audī|<u>rī</u>, numerā|rī* (ll. 39, 45), but consonant-verbs have only *-ī,* e.g. *em|<u>ī</u>: Sine pecūniā cibus emī nōn potest* (l. 62).

In this chapter the infinitive occurs as object of *potest possunt,* of *vult volunt,* the verb that denotes will (*Iūlia cum puerīs lūdere <u>vult</u>, neque iī cum puellā lūdere <u>volunt</u>,* ll.75-76), and of the verb *audet audent,* which denotes courage (*avēs canere nōn <u>audent</u>,* l. 88). It occurs also as subject of the <u>impersonal</u> expression *necesse est;* here the person for whom it is necessary to do something is in the dative (<u>dative of interest</u>): *spīrāre necesse est hominī* (l. 58).

The object of verbs of perception, like *vidēre* and *audīre,* can be combined with an infinitive to express what someone is seen or heard to be doing (active infinitive) or what is being done to someone (passive infinitive): *Puerī puell<u>am</u> can<u>ere</u> audiunt* (l. 80); *Aemilia fīli<u>um</u> su<u>um</u> ā Iūliō portā<u>rī</u> videt* (l. 126); *Aemilia Quīnt<u>um</u> ā Iūliō in lectō pōn<u>ī</u> aspicit* (l. 131).

The original ending of the infinitive was *-se;* but an intervocalic *-s-,* i.e. an *-s-* between vowels, was changed to *-r-,* so *-se* became *-re* after a vowel. Only in the infinitives *esse* (to *est sunt*) and *ēsse* (to *ēst edunt*) was the ending *-se* kept, because it was added directly to the stems *es-* and *ed-: es|se* and (with assimilation *ds >ss*) *ēs|se.* Examples: *Quī spīrat mortuus <u>esse</u> nōn potest* (l. 109); *<u>Ēsse</u> quoque hominī necesse est* (l. 59); *nēmō gemmās <u>ēsse</u> potest* (l. 64, where you also find the passive infinitive *edī* of *ēsse: Gemmae edī nōn possunt*).

Besides <u>means</u> and <u>cause</u> the simple ablative can also denote <u>manner</u> *(ablātīvus modī),* e.g. *magn<u>ā</u> vōc<u>e</u> clāmat* (l. 112); *'leō' dēclīnātur h<u>ōc</u> mod<u>ō</u>...*

20

Chapter 11

The art of healing was naturally far more primitive in the ancient world than it is today, although not all the doctors of antiquity were so incompetent as the zealous physician who treats poor Quintus.

Among the names of parts of the body there are a number of neuter nouns of the 3rd declension, e.g. *ōs, crūs, corpus, pectus, cor, iecur*. Like all neuters these nouns have the same form in the nominative and accusative, with the plural ending in *-a*. In the other cases they have the well-known endings of the 3rd declension. Note that a final *-s* is changed into *r* when endings are added: *ōs ōr|is, crūs crūr|is, corpus corpor|is, pectus pector|is* (in the last two, and in *iecur iecor|is,* the preceding vowel is changed from *u* to *o*). Irregular forms are *caput capit|is* and *cor cord|is; viscer|a -um* is only used in the plural. These nouns are all consonant-stems, like *flūmen -in|is,* and in the plural they have *-a* (nom./acc.) and *-um* (gen.). Examples of *i*-stems are *mar|e mar|is* and *animal -āl|is,* which in the plural have *-ia* (nom./acc.) and *-ium* (gen.) and in the ablative singular *-ī.* The complete declension patterns, or <u>paradigms</u>, are shown on page 83.

In sentences like *Iūlius puerum videt* and *Iūlius puerum audit* we have seen that an infinitive may be added to the accusative *puerum* to describe what the boy is doing or what is happening to him, e.g. *Iūlius puer<u>um</u> vocā<u>re</u> audit* and *Iūlius puer<u>um</u> perterritum esse videt*. Such an <u>accusative and infinitive</u> (Latin *accūsātīvus cum īnfīnītīvō*), where the accusative is logically the subject of the infinitive ('subject accusative'), is used in Latin not only with verbs of perceiving, like *vidēre, audīre* and *sentīre,* but with many other verbs, e.g. *iubēre (dominus serv<u>um</u> venī<u>re</u> iubet),* and with *dīcere* and *putāre* (and other verbs of saying and thinking) to report a person's words or thoughts as an <u>indirect statement</u>. Thus the doctor's words *"Puer dormit"* are rendered by Aemilia: *Medicus 'puer<u>um</u> dormī<u>re</u>' dīcit* (ll. 63-64, single quotation marks '...' denote reported or <u>indirect speech</u>); and the terrible thought that strikes Syra when she sees the unconscious Quintus is reported in this way: *Syra e<u>um</u> mortu<u>um</u> esse putat* (l. 108). The accusative and infinitive (acc. + inf.) is also found with *gaudēre* (and with other verbs expressing <u>mood</u>): *Syra Quīnt<u>um</u> vī<u>ve</u>re gaudet* (l. 118, = *Syra gaudet quod Quīntus vīvit*), and with *necesse est* (and other <u>impersonal</u> expressions): *Necesse est puer<u>um</u> aegr<u>um</u> dormī<u>re</u>* (l. 128). (In English indirect statement is generally expressed by a clause beginning with 'that': 'says/thinks/believes that...').

The conjunction *atque* (< *ad-que,* 'and... too') has the same function as *et* and *-que;* before consonants, but not before vowels or *h*-, the shortened form *ac* is often found (see cap. 12, l. 59). In this chapter (l. 54) you meet the shortened form *nec* of *neque;* it is used before consonants as well as vowels.

Like *ab* the preposition *dē* expresses motion 'from' (mostly 'down from') and takes the ablative: *dē arbore, dē bracchiō* (ll. 53, 99).

The ablatives *pede* and *capite* in *Nec modo pede, sed etiam capite aeger est* (l. 55, cf. ll. 131-132) specifies the application of the term *aeger*. It is called <u>ablative of respect</u>, as it answers the question 'in what respect?'

The infinitive of *potest possunt* is *posse,* as appears from the acc. + inf. stating Aemilia's low opinion of the doctor's competence: *Aemilia nōn putat medicum puerum aegrum sānāre posse* (ll. 134-135).

Speaking of her and Julius's son Aemilia says *fīlius <u>noster</u>* (l. 131); in cap. 12 you will find several examples of the <u>possessive pronouns</u> *noster -tra -trum* and *vester -tra -trum* referring to more than one owner (English 'our', 'your').

3rd decl. neuter

	sing.	plur.
nom.	-	*-a*
acc.	-	*-a*
gen.	*-is*	*-um*
dat.	*-ī*	*-ibus*
abl.	*-e*	*-ibus*

plural (nom./acc., gen.)
cons.-stems: *-a, -um*
i-stems: *-ia, -ium*

abl. sing.
cons.-stems: *-e*
i-stems: *-ī*

accusative & infinitive
(acc. + inf.) with
(1) *vidēre, audīre, sentīre*
(2) *iubēre*
(3) *dīcere*
(4) *putāre*
(5) *gaudēre*
(6) *necesse est*

M.: *"Puer dormit"*
M. *'puer<u>um</u> dormī<u>re</u>'
dīcit*

"..." = direct speech
'...' = indirect speech
(reported speech)

atque (< *ad-que*) = *et*
ac (+ cons.) = *atque*

nec = neque

dē prep. + abl. (↓)

ablative of respect:
pede aeger

ind. *potest possunt*
inf. *posse*

possessive pronouns
noster -tra -trum
vester -tra -trum

Chapter 12

The military played an important part in the Roman world. Above this chapter you find a picture of a *mīles Rōmānus*. The word 'military' is derived from *mīles*, whose stem ends in *-t:* gen. *mīlit|is* (so also *pedes -it|is* and *eques -i|tis*). Here you read about the equipment of a Roman soldier and the layout of a Roman army camp: *castra*. This noun is neuter <u>plural</u>; accordingly you read *castra <u>sunt</u>, vāllum castr<u>ōrum</u>, in castrīs* (ll. 93, 94, 101) though only one camp

plurale tantum:
castra -ōrum n. pl.

is meant. Like *līberī -ōrum, viscera -um* and *arma -ōrum* the noun *castra -ōrum* is a so-called *plūrāle tantum* ('plural only', cf. 'barracks', 'entrails', 'arms').

possessive dative
+ esse

In the sentence *Mārcō ūna soror est* (l. 6) *Mārc<u>ō</u>* is dative. This could also be expressed *Mārcus ūnam sorōrem habet*; but *ūna soror* is nominative, and the dative *Mārcō* tells us 'to whom' or 'for whom' there is a sister. Such a <u>possessive dative</u> with *esse* is used to express to whom something belongs; cf. *Quod nōmen est patrī? <u>Eī</u> nōmen est Lūcius Iūlius Balbus* (ll. 9-10).

Roman names:
praenōmen
nōmen
cognōmen

Iūlius is a <u>family name</u>: male members of this family are called *Iūlius* and female members *Iūlia*. Besides the family name in *-ius* Roman men have a first or personal name, *praenōmen* (see the list in the margin of p. 86), and a surname, *cognōmen*, which is common to a branch of the family. The *cognōmen* is often descriptive of the founder of the family, e.g. *Longus, Pulcher, Crassus; Paulus* means 'small' and *Balbus* 'stammering'.

4th declension

	sing.	plur.
nom.	*-us*	*-ūs*
acc.	*-um*	*-ūs*
gen.	*-ūs*	*-uum*
dat.	*-uī*	*-ibus*
abl.	*-ū*	*-ibus*

The noun *exercitus* here represents the <u>4th declension</u> (*dēclīnātiō quārta*). All the forms are shown in ll. 80–89: in the singular the accusative has *-um*, the genitive *-ūs*, the dative *-uī*, and the ablative *-ū*; in the plural the nominative and accusative end in *-ūs*, the genitive in *-uum*, the dative and ablative in *-ibus*. 4th declension nouns are regularly masculine, e.g. *arcus, equitātus, exercitus, impetus, metus, passus, versus; manus* is feminine (*duae manūs*). This declension does not comprise nearly so many words as the first three.

imperāre, pārēre + dat.

In the sentences *Dux exercituī imperat* and *Exercitus ducī suō pāret* (l. 82) *exercituī* and *ducī* are datives. This shows that the verbs *imperāre* and *pārēre* take the dative (persons whom you command and whom you obey are in the dative). You will soon find more verbs that take the dative.

3rd decl. adjectives

sing.	m./f.	n.
nom.	*-is*	*-e*
acc.	*-em*	*-e*
gen.	*-is*	
dat./abl.	*-ī*	
plur.		
nom./acc.	*-ēs*	*-ia*
gen.	*-ium*	
dat./abl.	*-ibus*	

All the adjectives learned so far, e.g. *alb|us -a -um*, follow the 1st and 2nd declensions: the 1st in the feminine *(alb|a)* and the 2nd in the masculine and neuter *(alb|us, alb|um)* – a few, like *niger -gr|a -gr|um*, have *-er*, not *-us*, in the nom. sing. m., thus *aeger, pulcher, ruber* and *noster, vester* (cf. nouns like *liber -br|ī, culter -tr|ī*). Now you meet <u>adjectives of the 3rd declension</u>, namely *brevis, gravis, levis, trīstis, fortis, tenuis* already appeared in cap. 10. In the masculine and feminine they are declined like *ovis*, except that in the ablative they take *-ī* (not *-e*); in the neuter they are declined like *mare* (i.e. in the nom./acc. they have *-e* in the singular and *-ia* in the plural). So in the nominative singular we have *gladius brev<u>is</u>, hasta brev<u>is</u>* and *pīlum brev<u>e</u>*.

comparative

sing.	m./f.	n.
nom.	*-ior*	*-ius*
acc.	*-iōrem*	*-ius*
gen.	*-iōris*	
dat.	*-iōrī*	
abl.	*-iōre*	
plur.		
nom./acc.	*-iōrēs*	*-iōra*
gen.	*-iōrum*	
dat./abl.	*-iōribus*	

A comparison like *Via Latīna nōn tam longa est quam via Appia* can also be expressed: *Via Appia long<u>ior</u> est quam Latīna*. *Longior* is a <u>comparative</u> (*comparātīvus*, from *comparāre*, 'compare'). The comparative ends in *-ior* in the masculine and feminine and in *-ius* in the neuter (*gladius/hasta longior, pīlum long<u>ius</u>*) and follows the 3rd declension: gen. *-iōr|is*, plur. nom./acc. *-iōr|ēs* (m./f.) and *-iōr|a* (n.); abl. sing. *-e* (not *-ī*): *-iōr|e*. Examples: ll. 53, 58-59, 127, 130, 134-135, and in the section GRAMMATICA LATINA ll. 200–225.

partitive genitive

The genitives in *Prōvincia est pars imperiī Rōmānī, ut membrum pars corporis est* (ll. 64-65) indicate the whole of which a part (*pars part|is* f.) is taken. It is called <u>partitive genitive</u>. Cf. the genitive in *magnus numerus mīlit<u>um</u>*.

22

The common Roman linear measures were *pēs,* 'foot' (29.6 cm), and *passus* = 5 *pedēs* (1.48 m); *mīlle passūs* (4th decl.), a 'Roman mile' of 1.48 km, is a little less than an English mile. The plural of *mīlle* is *mīlia -ium* n., e.g. *duo mīlia* (2000), which is followed by a partitive genitive: *duo mīlia passuum; sex mīlia mīlitum.* Long distances were given in *mīlia passuum* ('Roman miles', 'mile' is derived from *mīlia*). The accusative is used to indicate extent ('how long?' 'how high?'), e.g. *Gladius duōs pedēs longus est.*

5 *pedēs* = 1 *passus*

mīlia + gen. plur.

Besides consonant-stems (like *pōn|ere, sūm|ere, dīc|ere*) the 3rd conjugation comprises some verbs whose stems end in short *u* or *i.* The inflection of *u*-stems, e.g. *flu|ere* and *metu|ere,* does not differ from that of consonant-stems. In the *i*-stems *i* changes into *e* before *r,* e.g. in the infinitive: *cape|re, iace|re, fuge|re,* stem *capi-, iaci-, fugi-,* and in final position: *cape! iace! fuge!* (imperative); so *i*-stems, too, largely agree with consonant-stems, but they are characterized by having *i* before vowel endings, e.g. *-unt: capi|unt, iaci|unt, fugi|unt* (cf. *accipiunt* and *aspiciunt* in cap. 8, inf. *accipere, aspicere*).

verbal *u*- and *i*-stems

In the verb *fer|re* (l. 55) the infinitive ending *-re* is added directly to the consonant-stem *fer-;* so are the endings *-t* and *-tur: fer|t, fer|tur* (ll. 34, 57, plur. *fer|unt, fer|untur*) and the imperative has no *-e: fer!* (plur. *fer|te!*). Cf. the short imperatives *es!* of esse (plur. *es|te!*) and *dūc!* of *dūcere* (plur. *dūc|ite!*). Two more 3rd conjugation verbs, *dīcere* and *facere,* have no *-e* in the imperative singular: *dīc! fac!* (plur. *dīc|ite! faci|te! – facere* is an *i*-stem: *faci|unt*).

inf. *fer|re*
ind. *fer|t   fer|unt*
      fer|tur fer|untur
imp. *fer!   fer|te!*

imp. *dīc! dūc! fac! fer!*

Chapter 13

Today we still use the Roman calendar, as it was reformed by Julius Caesar in 46 B.C., with twelve months and 365 days (366 in leap years). Before this reform, only four months – March, May, July and October – had 31 days, while February had 28, and the other months only 29. This made a total of 355 days. It was therefore necessary at intervals to put in an extra month!

the Roman calendar

The noun *diēs,* gen. *diēī,* here represents the 5th declension (Latin *dēclīnātiō quīnta*). The complete paradigm is shown on page 101. 5th declension nouns have stems in *ē,* which is kept before all endings (but shortened in *-em*). The number of these nouns is very small; most of them have *-iēs* in the nominative, like *diēs, merīdiēs, faciēs, glaciēs:* a few have a consonant before *-ēs* (and short *e* in gen./dat. sing. *-eī*), e.g. the common word *rēs,* gen. *reī* ('thing', 'matter'), which turns up in the next chapter. The nouns of this declension are feminine except *diēs* (and *merī-diēs*) which is masculine (in special senses and in Late Latin it is feminine).

5th declension
      sing.   plur.
nom. *-ēs   -ēs*
acc. *-em   -ēs*
gen *-eī/-eī -ērum*
dat. *-eī/-eī -ēbus*
abl. *-ē   -ēbus*

*merī-diē < medi-diē
(mediō diē)*

You have now learned all five declensions. The classification is based on the (original) final stem-vowel:

1st declension: *a*-stems, e.g. *āla,* gen. sing. *-ae*
2nd declension: *o*-stems, e.g. *equus, ōvum < equo|s, ōvo|m,* gen. sing. *-ī* (< *-oi*)
3rd declension: consonant-stems and *i*-stems, e.g. *sōl, ovi|s,* gen. sing. *-is*
4th declension: *u*-stems, e.g. *lacu|s,* gen. sing. *-ūs*
5th declension: *ē*-stems, e.g. *diē|s, rē|s,* gen. sing. *-ēī, -eī.*

The neuter noun *māne* is indeclinable (ll. 36, 37; cf. cap. 14, l. 55).

1st decl.: *a*-stems
  gen. *-ae*
2nd decl.: *o*-stems
  gen. *-ī*
3rd decl.: cons./i-stems
  gen. *-is*
4th decl.: *u*-stems
  gen. *-ūs*
5th decl.: *ē*-stems
  gen. *-ēī/-eī*

The names of the months are adjectives: *mēnsis Iānuārius,* etc., but they are often used alone without *mēnsis. Aprīlis* and *September, Octōber, November, December* are 3rd declension adjectives, so they have ablative in *-ī: (mense) Aprīlī, Septembrī, Octōbrī,* etc. Note: nom. m. *-ber* (without *-is*), gen. *-br|is.*

23

question: 'when?' 'how long?'	answer: abl. acc.

cardinals:
ūnus, duo, trēs...
ordinals:
prīmus, secundus, tertius...

To express 'time <u>when</u>' the ablative *(ablātīvus temporis)* is used: *mēnse Decembrī, illō tempore, hōrā prīmā, merīdiē, hieme.* 'Time <u>how long</u>' (duration) is expressed by the accusative: *centum annōs vīvere* (l. 11).

Of the Latin <u>numerals</u> you know the <u>cardinals</u> 1–10 *(ūnus, duo... decem)* and the <u>ordinals</u> 1st–4th: *prīmus, secundus, tertius, quārtus.* In numbering the months the first twelve ordinals are needed: *prīmus... duodecimus* (ll. 2–6). The ordinals are combined with *pars* to form <u>fractions</u>: 1/3 *tertia pars,* 1/4 *quārta pars,* 1/5 *quīnta pars* etc., but 1/2 *dīmidia pars* (ll. 33-34).

In the oldest Roman calendar March was the first month of the year. This explains the names *September, Octōber, November* and *December* (< *septem, octō, novem, decem).* The fifth month in the old calendar was called *Quīntilis* (< *quīntus),* but after the death of Julius Caesar it was named *Iūlius* in memory of him. In the year 8 B.C. the following month, which until then had been called *Sextīlis* (< *sextus),* was given the name of the Roman emperor *Augustus.*

present tense: *est sunt*
past tense: *erat erant*

The forms *erat erant* are used instead of *est sunt* when the past is concerned. Compare the sentences: *tempore antīquō Mārtius mēnsis prīmus erat. Tunc (= illō tempore) September mēnsis septimus erat* (ll. 19-20) and *Nunc (= hōc tempore) mēnsis prīmus est Iānuārius* (l. 22). *Erat erant* is called the <u>past tense</u> or <u>preterite</u>, while *est sunt* is the <u>present tense</u> ('tense' comes from Latin *tempus).* The past tense of other verbs comes later (from cap. 19).

In the example *Februārius brevior est quam Iānuārius* a comparison is made between the two months: *brevior* is the <u>comparative</u> of *brevis.* In the sentence *Februārius mēnsis annī brevissimus est* (l. 30) February is compared with all the other months of the year, none of which is as short as February: *brevissimus* is the <u>superlative</u> (Latin *superlātīvus)* of *brevis.*

<u>superlative</u>

comparison (degrees)
1. pos.: *-us -a -um /-is -e*
2. comp.: *-ior -ius -iōr|is*
3. sup.: *-issim|us -a -um*

You have now learned the three <u>degrees</u> of <u>comparison</u>:
1. <u>Positive</u>: *-us -a -um, -is -e,* e.g. *longus -a -um, brevis -e.*
2. <u>Comparative</u> ('higher degree'): *-ior -ius,* e.g. *longior -ius.*
3. <u>Superlative</u> ('highest degree'): *-issimus -a -um,* e.g. *longissimus -a -um.*

	March	all
	May	the
	July	other
	Oct.	months
1st	*kalendae*	
5th		*nōnae*
7th	*nōnae*	
13th		*īdūs*
15th	*īdūs*	

Three days in each month had special names: *kalendae* the 1st, *īdūs* the 13th, and *nōnae* the 5th (the 9th day before *īdūs:* inclusive reckoning); but in March, May, July and October (the four months that originally had 31 days) *īdūs* was the 15th and *nōnae* consequently the 7th. To these names, which are feminine plurals *(īdūs -uum* 4th decl.), the names of the months are added as adjectives. Thus January 1st is *kalendae Iānuāriae,* January 5th *nōnae Iānuāriae,* and January 13th *īdūs Iānuāriae.* Dates are given in the *ablātīvus temporis,* e.g. *kalendīs Iānuāriīs* 'on January 1st' and *īdibus Mārtiīs* 'on March 15th'.

Other dates were indicated by stating the number of days before the following *kalendae, nōnae* or *īdūs.* April 21st (Rome's birthday) is the 11th day before *kalendae Māiae* (inclusive reckoning!), it should therefore be *diēs ūndecimus ante kalendās Māiās,* but *ante* being illogically put first it became *ante diem ūndecimum kalendās Māiās* (shortened *a. d. XI kal. Māi.*).

a. d. = ante diem

nom.+ inf.+ *dīcitur*

Note the passive *dīcitur* with an infinitive: *lūna 'nova' esse dīcitur* (l. 52, nom. + inf., 'is said to be..'; cf. *(hominēs) lūnam 'novam' esse dīcunt:* acc.+ inf.). Elsewhere *dīcitur = nōminātur* ('is called', e.g. ll. 58, 64, 69, 72, 77...).

ind. *vult volunt*
inf. *Velle*

The infinitive of *vult volunt* has the irregular form *velle,* as appears from the acc. + inf. in *Aemilia puerum dormīre velle putat* (l. 140). The conjunction

the conjunctions *vel* and *aut*

vel is originally the imperative of *velle;* it implies a free choice between two expressions or possibilities: *XII mēnsēs vel CCCLXV diēs; centum annī vel saeculum; hōra sexta vel merīdiēs* (ll. 7, 9, 43) – as distinct from *aut,* which is put between mutually exclusive alternatives: *XXVIII aut XXIX diēs* (l. 28).

24

Chapter 14

At dawn Marcus is roused from his morning slumbers by Davus, who also sees to it that he washes properly before putting on his *tunica* and *toga,* the clothes that were the mark of freeborn Roman men and boys.

Among the new words in this chapter you should pay particular attention to *uter, neuter, alter* and *uterque.* These pronouns are used only when two persons or things are concerned. *Uter utra utrum* is the interrogative pronoun used where there are only two alternatives ('which of the two?'), e.g. *Uter puer, Mārcusne an Quīntus?* (the conjunction *an,* not *aut,* is put between the two in question). The answer may be:

(1) *neuter -tra -trum* ('neither'), e.g. *neuter puer, nec Mārcus nec Quīntus;*
(2) *alter -era -erum* ('one'/'the other'), e.g. *alter puer, aut M. aut Q.;*
(3) *uter- utra- utrum-que* ('each of the two'), e.g. *uterque puer, et M. et Q.*

question:
uter utra utrum?
A-ne an B?
answer:
neuter -tra -trum:
  nec A nec B
alter -era -erum:
  aut A aut B
uter- utra- utrum-que:
  et A et B

Where English prefers 'both' followed by the plural ('both boys'), Latin has the singular *uterque.* Even if there are two subjects separated by *neque... neque, aut... aut* or *et... et* the verb is in the singular, as in *et caput et pēs eī dolet* (ll. 3-4) and *nec caput nec pēs dolet* (l. 66). The general rule is that two or more subjects take a verb in the plural if they denote persons, but if the subjects are things the verb agrees with the nearest subject, as in *pēs et caput eī dolet* (l. 64). – Note here the dative *eī,* which is called dative of interest (*datīvus commodī*); it denotes the person concerned, benefited or harmed; cf. the sentence *Multīs barbarīs magna corporis pars nūda est* (l. 77).

uterque sing.

dative of interest

The ablative of *duo duae duo* is: masculine and neuter *duōbus (ē duōbus puerīs; in duōbus cubiculīs)* and feminine *duābus (ē duābus fenestrīs).*

      m./n.   f.
nom. *duo*   *duae*
abl. *duōbus* *duābus*

On page 104 a new form of the *verb* is introduced, the so-called participle (Latin *participium*) ending in *-(e)ns: puer dormiēns* = *puer quī dormit, puer vigilāns* = *puer quī vigilat.* The participle is a 3rd declension adjective: *vigilāns,* gen. *-ant|is, dormiēns,* gen. *-ent|is (-ns* also neuter nom./acc. sing.: *caput dolēns),* but it keeps verbal functions, e. g. it may take an object in the accusative: *Dāvus cubiculum intrāns interrogat...* (l. 25). This form, being part verb and part adjective, was called *participium* (< *pars partis*). As a verb form the participle usually has *-e* in the ablative singular, e. g. *Parentēs ā fīliō intrante salūtantur* (l. 91) – only when used as a pure adjective has it *-ī.*

participle
          m./f.   n.
nom   *-ns*   *-ns*
acc.   *-ntem*   *-ns*
gen.   *-ntis*
dat.   *-ntī*
abl.   *-nte/-ntī*
plur.
nom./acc. *-ntēs*   *-ntia*
gen.   *-ntium*
dat./abl.   *-ntibus*

The datives corresponding to the accusatives *mē, tē* are *mihi, tibi: "Affer mihi aquam...!"* and *"Dā mihi tunicam...!"* says Quintus (ll. 43, 71); when Marcus says: *"Mihi quoque caput dolet!"* he is told by Davus: *"Tibi nec caput nec pēs dolet!"* (ll. 65-66, dative of interest, cf. ll. 64, 86, 103). The ablative of these pronouns is identical with the accusative: *mē, tē.* The preposition *cum* is suffixed to these forms: *mē-cum, tē-cum;* similarly *sē-cum: Dāvus... eum sēcum venīre iubet: "Venī mēcum!"* (ll. 86-87); *"Mēdus tēcum īre nōn potest"* (l. 117, cf. ll. 108, 120, 128).

acc. *mē*   *tē*
dat. *mihi* *tibi*
abl. *mē*   *tē*

mē-cum
tē-cum
sē-cum

The verb *inquit,* '(he/she) says', is inserted after one or more words of direct speech: *"Hōra prīma est" inquit Dāvus, "Surge ē lectō!"* (l. 40); *Servus Mārcō aquam affert et "Ecce aqua" inquit* (l. 44). It is a defective verb: only *inquit inquiunt* and a few other forms of the indicative occur.

"...." inquit "....."

The opposite of *nūllus* is *omnis -e* ('every', 'all'), which more often appears in the plural *omnēs -ia* (see ll. 115, 119). Used without a noun the plural *omnēs* ('everybody') is the opposite of *nēmō* ('nobody') and the neuter plural *omnia* ('everything') is the opposite of *nihil* ('nothing').

omnis ↔ *nūllus*
omnēs ↔ *nēmō*
omnia ↔ *nihil*

Chapter 15

Rome had no public school system. Parents who could afford it sent their young children to an elementary school, *lūdus*. It was run as a private enterprise by a *lūdī magister*, who taught the children reading, writing and arithmetic. We now follow Marcus to school. His teacher tries his best to maintain discipline, but he has some difficulty in keeping these boys in hand.

1st person (1.)
2nd person (2.)
3rd person (3.)

personal endings
sing. plur.
1. -ō   -mus
2. -s   -tis
3. -t   -nt (-unt)

3rd conjugation
sing. plur.
1. -ō   -imus
2. -is   -itis
3. -it   -unt

From the conversation between the teacher and his pupils you learn that the verbs have different endings according as one speaks about oneself (1st person), adresses another person (2nd person), or speaks about someone else (3rd person). When Titus says: *"Mārcus meum librum habet"*, the teacher asks Marcus: *"Quid* (= *cūr*) *tū librum Titī habēs?"* and he answers: *"Ego eius librum habeō, quod is meum mālum habet"* (ll. 85–88). It appears from this that in the singular the 1st person of the verb ends in -ō (*habe|ō*), the 2nd in -s (*habe|s*), and the 3rd, as you know, in -t (*habe|t*). In the plural the 1st person ends in -mus, the 2nd in -tis, the 3rd in -nt. Addressing Sextus and Titus Marcus says: *"Vōs iānuam nōn pulsātis, cum ad lūdum venītis"* (ll. 51-52) and they answer: *"Nōs iānuam pulsāmus, cum ad lūdum venīmus"* (l. 55). So *pulsā|mus, venī|mus* is the 1st person plural, and *pulsā|tis, venī|tis* the 2nd person plural. The examples on page 112 (ll. 45–58) and in the section GRAMMATICA LATINA show how these personal endings are added to the various stems in the present tense. Note that *ā* is dropped, and *ē* and *ī* shortened, before -ō: *puls|ō, habe|ō, veni|ō* (stems *pulsā-, habē-, venī-*) and that in consonant-stems a short *i* is inserted before -s, -mus and -tis just as before -t: *dīc|is, dīc|imus, dīc|itis* (stem *dīc-*). Under the 3rd conjugation the verb *facere* is included as an example of a verb whose stem ends in a short *i*, which appears before the endings -ō and -unt: *faci|ō, faci|unt*. Other verbs of this kind are *accipere, aspicere, capere, fugere, iacere, incipere, parere.*

faci|ō faci|unt

personal pronouns
nominative
sing. plur.
1. ego   nōs
2. tū   vōs

The verbs in the above examples are preceded by personal pronouns in the nominative: *ego, tū* (1st and 2nd pers. sing.) and *nōs, vōs* (1st and 2nd pers. plur.). But these pronouns are only used when the subject is emphasized; normally the personal ending is sufficient to show which person is meant, as in the teacher's question to Titus: *"Cūr librum nōn habēs?"* and Titus's answer: *"Librum nōn habeō, quod..."* (ll. 38-39). The accusative of *ego* and *tū* is *mē* and *tē*, but *nōs* and *vōs* are the same in the accusative: *"Quid nōs verberās, magister?"* *"Vōs verberō, quod..."* (ll. 119-120). – The missing genitive of the personal pronouns is replaced by the possessive pronouns: *meus, tuus* (1st and 2nd pers. sing.), *noster, vester* (1st and 2nd pers. plur.).

possessive pronouns
sing. plur.
1. meus   noster
2. tuus   vester

esse sing. plur.
1. sum   sumus
2. es   estis
3. est   sunt
posse
1. pos-sum pos-sumus
2. pot-es   pot-estis
3. pot-est pos-sunt

The verb *esse* is irregular. Corresponding to the 3rd person *est* and *sunt* the 1st person is *sum* and *sumus*, the 2nd *es* and *estis*: *"Cūr tū sōlus es, Sexte?"* *"Ego sōlus sum, quod..."* (ll. 20-21); *"Ubi estis, puerī?"* *"In lūdō sumus"* (ll. 113-114). The verb *posse* and other compounds of *esse* show the same irregular forms: *pos-sum, pot-es, pos-sumus, pot-estis* (*pot-* > *pos-* before *s*).

Q.: *"(Ego) aeger sum"*
Q. *'sē aegrum esse'*
dīcit

Quīntus's words: *"(Ego) aeger sum"* are reported by Marcus: *Quīntus dīcit 'sē aegrum esse'* (l. 82). When reporting in acc. + inf. (indirect speech) what a person says in the 1st person, the subject accusative is the reflexive *sē.* Cf. *Dāvus... eum sēcum venīre iubet: "Venī mēcum!"* (cap. 14, l. 87).

acc. of exclamation

The accusative is used in exclamations like the teacher's *"Ō, discipulōs improbōs...!"* (l. 23). In exclamations addressed to persons present the vocative is used: *"Ō improbī discipulī!"* (l. 101; in the plural voc. = nom.).

impersonal verb:
licet (+ dat.)

The verb *licet* ('it is allowed', 'one may') is impersonal, i.e. only found in the 3rd person singular. It is often combined with a dative: *mihi licet* ('I may').

Chapter 16

When sailing on the high seas the Roman sailor had to set his course by the sun in the daytime and by the stars at night. So east and west are named in Latin after the rising and the setting sun, *oriēns* and *occidēns*, and the word for 'midday', *merīdiēs*, also means 'south', while the word for 'north' is the name of the constellation *septentriōnēs* (*septem triōnēs*), 'the seven plow-oxen', i.e. 'the Great Bear'.

Many of the new words in this chapter are found only in the passive (infinitive *-rī*, *-ī*, 3rd person *-tur*, *-ntur*), e.g. *laetārī, verērī, sequī, opperīrī*. These verbs have no active form (apart from forms not found in the passive, like the participle in *-ns*) and are called <u>deponent verbs</u> (*verba dēpōnentia*), i.e. verbs which 'lay down' the active form (Latin *dēpōnere*, 'lay down'). In meaning they conform to active verbs; they are said to be <u>passive in form</u>, but <u>active in meaning</u>: *laetārī* = *gaudēre; opperīrī* = *exspectāre; nautae Neptū-num verētur* = *timet; ventō secundō nāvēs ē portū ēgrediuntur* = *exeunt.*

deponent verbs
passive form:
inf. *-rī, -ī*
3rd pers.: *-tur, -ntur*
active meaning:
laetārī = *gaudēre*
verērī = *timēre*
ēgredī = *exīre*
opperīrī = *exspectāre*

In the last example (ll. 38-39) the ablative *ventō secundō* tells us <u>under what circumstances</u> the ships put out ('with a fair wind', 'when the wind is favorable'). The ablatives in l. 36 have a similar function: *Nautae nec marī turbidō nec marī tranquillō nāvigāre volunt; cf. plēnīs vēlīs* (ll. 39-40), and *fenestrā apertā* and *pedibus nūdīs* (cap. 14, ll. 15, 85). This use of the ablative, which may often be translated with an English temporal clause, is called <u>ablative absolute</u> (Latin *ablātīvus absolūtus*, 'set free', because it is grammatically independent of the rest of the sentence). It often occurs with a participle: *Sōle oriente nāvis ē portū ēgreditur multīs hominibus spectantibus* (ll. 64-65; 'when the sun is rising', 'at sunrise' ... 'while many people are looking on'). Even two nouns can form an ablative absolute: *Sōle duce nāvem gubernō* (l. 94; 'the sun being my guide', 'with the sun as a guide').

ablative absolute: 'under what circumstances'

noun + adjective

noun + participle

noun + noun

The chapter begins: *Italia inter duo maria interest, quōrum alterum...'mare Superum'... appellātur; quōrum* (= *ex quibus*) is the <u>partitive genitive</u> of the relative pronoun; cf. *nēmō eōrum* (= *ex iīs*, cap. 17, l. 12). Quantity terms like *multum* and *paulum* are often followed by a partitive genitive to express 'that of which' there is a large or small quantity, e.g. *paulum/multum aquae* (ll. 8-9, 117), *paulum cibī nec multum pecūniae* (ll. 61-62), *paulum temporis* (l. 108 margin). Cf. the partitive genitive with *(magnus/parvus) numerus* and *mīlia*.

partitive genitive

multum, paulum
+ partitive gen.

The ablative of *multum* and *paulum* serves to strengthen or weaken a comparative: *Nāvis paulō levior fit, simul verō flūctūs multō altiōrēs fīunt* (ll. 123-124). This ablative is used with *ante* and *post* (as adverbs) to state the time difference: *paulō ante; paulō post* (ll. 91,148); cf. the ablative in *annō post; decem annīs post/ante* (cap. 19, ll. 83,86,123); it is called <u>ablative of difference</u>.

multō | *-ior -ius*
paulō | *ante*
       | *post*

ablative of difference

The ablative (locative) of *locus* may be used without *in* to denote location: *eō locō* (l. 16) = *in eō locō*. In the expression *locō movēre* (l. 140) the ablative without a preposition denotes motion 'from' (= *ē locō*): ablative of separation.

ablative of separation:
locō movēre

The noun *puppis -is* (f.) is a pure *i*-stem, which has *-im* in the accusative and *-ī* in the ablative singular (instead of *-em* and *-e*: see ll. 41, 67). Very few *i*-stems are declined in this way, e.g. the river name *Tiberis -is* m. (ll. 7, 9).

nom. *puppis*
acc. *puppim*
abl. *puppī*

1st declension nouns (in *-a -ae*) are feminine, except for a few which denote male persons and are therefore masculine, e.g. *nauta: nauta Rōmānus.*

nauta -ae m.

Irregular verb forms are the 1st person *eō* of *īre* (l. 72; cf. *eunt*) and the infinitive *fi|erī* (3rd person *fi|t fī|unt*). This verb functions as the passive of *facere* (see cap. 18); in connection with an adjective it comes to mean 'become': *mare tranquillum fit* (l. 98); *flūctūs multō altiōrēs fīunt* (l. 124).

ī|re: e|ō, e|unt
fi|erī: fi|t, fī|unt

Chapter 17

Roman coins
as assis m.
sēstertius (HS) = 4 *assēs*
dēnārius = 4 *sēstertiī*
aureus = 25 *dēnāriī*

sēmis -issis m. *(sēs-)*
= ½ *as*

To teach his pupils arithmetic the teacher has recourse to coins. The current Roman coins were the *as* (*assis* m.), copper, the *sēstertius*, brass, the *dēnārius*, silver – and the *aureus*, gold (cap. 22, l. 108). The value of 1 *sēstertius* was 4 *assēs*, of 1 *dēnārius* 4 *sēstertiī*, and of 1 *aureus* 25 *dēnāriī*. Until 217 B.C. the *sēs-tertius* was a small silver coin worth 2½ *assēs*, hence the abbreviation IIS (S = *sēmis* ½), which became HS; the change to 4 *assēs* was due to a fall in the copper value of the *as* (originally 1 'pound', 327 g, of copper).

cardinals:
30–90 *-gintā*

To be able to count up to a hundred you must learn the multiples of ten. With the exception of 10 *decem* and 20 *vīgintī* they all end in *-gintā*: 30 *trīgintā*, 40 *quadrāgintā*, 50 *quīnquāgintā*, etc. The numbers in between are formed by combining multiples of ten and smaller numbers with or without *et*, e.g. 21 *vīgintī ūnus* or *ūnus et vīgintī*, 22 *vīgintī duo* or *duo et vīgintī*, etc.

11–17 *-decim*
18/19: *duo-/ūn-dē-XX*
28/29: *duo-/ūn-dē-XXX*
38/39: *duo-/ūn-dē-XL*
etc.

The cardinals 11–17 end in *-decim*, a weakened form of *decem:* 11 *ūn-decim*, 12 *duo-decim*, 13 *trē-decim* up to 17 *septen-decim;* but 18 is *duo-dē-vīgintī* and 19 *ūn-dē-vīgintī* ('two-from-twenty' and 'one-from-twenty'); in the same way 28 is *duo-dē-trīgintā* and 29 *ūn-dē-trīgintā.* Thus the last two numbers before each multiple of ten are expressed by subtracting 2 and 1 respectively from the multiple of ten in question.

Most Latin cardinals are indeclinable – like *quot*, the interrogative which asks the number ('how many?'), and *tot*, the demonstrative which refers to the number ('so many'). Of the cardinals 1–100 only *ūn|us -a -um, du|o -ae -o* and *tr|ēs tr|ia* are declined. You have met most forms of these numbers (the genitive, *ūn|īus, du|ōrum -ārum -ōrum* and *tr|ium,* is introduced in cap. 19).

200, 300, 600: *-cent|ī*
400, 500, 700, 800,
900: *-gent|ī*

Multiples of 100 *centum* end in *-centī* (200, 300, 600) or *-gentī* (400, 500, 700, 800, 900) and are declined like adjectives of the 1st/2nd declension: 200 *du-cent|ī -ae -a,* 300 *tre-cent|ī -ae -a,* 400 *quadrin-gent|ī -ae -a,* etc.

ordinals:
20th–90th, 100th–
1000th: *-ēsim|us*

The ordinals are adjectives of the 1st/2nd declension; from the multiples of ten, 20–90, and of one hundred, 100–1000, they are formed with the suffix *-ēsim|us -a -um:* 20th *vīcēsimus,* 30th *trīcēsimus,* 40th *quadrāgēsimus,* 50th *quīnquāgēsimus,* etc., and 100th *centēsimus,* 200th *ducentēsimus,* 300th *trecentēsimus,* etc. up to 1000th *mīllēsimus.* A survey is given on page 308.

passive
personal endings
	sing.	plur.
1.	*-or*	*-mur*
2	*-ris*	*-minī*
3.	*-tur*	*-ntur*

3rd conjugation
	sing.	plur.
1.	*-or*	*-imur*
2.	*-eris*	*-iminī*
3.	*-itur*	*-untur*

The active sentence *Magister Mārcum nōn laudat, sed reprehendit* becomes in the passive *Mārcus ā magistrō nōn laudātur, sed reprehenditur.* Marcus now asks his teacher: *"Cūr ego semper ā tē reprehendor, numquam laudor?"* and the teacher answers: *"Tū ā mē nōn laudāris, quia numquam rēctē respondēs. Semper prāvē respondēs, ergō reprehenderis!"* (ll. 63–68). *Laud|or, reprehend|or* and *laudā|ris, reprehend|eris* are the passive forms of the 1st and 2nd persons singular; in the plural the 1st person is *laudā|mur,* reprehend|imur* (Sextus says about himself and Titus: *"Nōs ā magistrō laudāmur, nōn reprehendimur"*) and the 2nd person *laudā|minī, reprehend|iminī.* The examples in the section GRAMMATICA LATINA show how the passive personal endings *-or, -mur* (1st pers.), *-ris, -minī* (2nd pers.) and *-tur, -ntur* (3rd pers.) are added to the various verbal stems. In consonant-stems *-i-* is inserted before *-mur* and *-minī (merg|imur, merg|iminī), -e-* before *-ris (merg|eris),* and *-u-* before *-ntur (merg|untur;* so also in *-ī-*stems: *audi|untur).*

docēre + double acc.

Note the two accusatives with *docēre: Magister puerōs numerōs docet* (l. 2).

The forms *rēctē, prāvē, stultē, aequē* are formed from the adjectives *rēctus, prāvus, stultus, aequus;* this formation will be dealt with in the next chapter.

da|re: stem *da-*

The stem of the verb *da|re* ends in a short *a: da|mus, da|tis, da|tur, da|te!* etc., except in *dā! dā|s* and *dā|ns* (before *ns* all vowels are lengthened).

28

Chapter 18

In the Classical period Latin spelling gave a fairly reliable representation of the pronunciation. In some cases, however, letters continued to be written where they were no longer pronounced in colloquial Latin, e.g. *h-*, *-m* in the unstressed endings *-am*, *-em*, *-um* and *n* before *s*. An indication of this is the occurrence of "misspellings" in ancient inscriptions written by people without literary education, e.g. ORA for HORAM, SEPTE for SEPTEM and MESES for MENSES. In his short exercise Marcus makes several errors of this kind.

Latin orthography

The demonstrative pronoun *īdem eadem idem* ('the same', cf. '<u>ident</u>ical') is a compound, the first element of which is the pronoun *is ea id;* the addition of the suffix *-dem* causes the change of *is-dem* to *īdem* and *eum-dem, eam-dem* to *eu<u>n</u>dem, ea<u>n</u>dem* (by assimilation, *n* being a dental consonant like *d*, cf. *septe<u>n</u>decim* and *septe<u>n</u>triōnēs*). The pronoun *quis-que quae-que quod-que* ('each') is declined like the interrogative pronoun with the addition of *-que*.

īdem < is-dem
eu<u>n</u>dem < eum-dem
ea<u>n</u>dem < eam-dem

Adjectives in *-er*, e.g. *pulcher* and *piger*, form superlatives in *-errim|us -a -um.* (istead of *-issimus*). In this chapter you find *pulcherrim|us* and *pigerrim|us* (ll. 73, 84), in the next (ll. 98, 128) *miserrim|us* and *pauperrim|us* from *miser* and *pauper*. The superlative of *facilis* is *facillim|us* (l. 102).

adj *-er*, sup. *-errim|us*

facil|is, sup. *-illim|us*

In the sentence *puer stul<u>tus</u> est, stultus* is an adjective qualifying the noun *puer* (it answers the question *quālis est puer?*). In the sentence *puer stul<u>tē</u> agit* the word *stultē* belongs to the verb *agit* which it qualifies (question: *quō-modo agit puer?*); such a word is called an <u>adverb</u> (Latin *adverbium*, from *ad verbum*). Similarly, in the sentence *mīles <u>fortis</u> est quī <u>fortiter</u> pugnat, fortis* is an adjective (qualifying *mīles*) and *fortiter* an adverb (qualifying *pugnat*). Adjectives of the 1st/2nd declension, e.g. *stult|us -a -um, rēct|us -a -um, pulcher -chr|a -chr|um,* form adverbs in *-ē: stultē, rēctē, pulchrē* (*bene* and *male* are irregular formations from *bonus* and *malus*). 3rd declension adjectives, e.g. *fort|is -e, brev|is -e, turp|is -e,* form adverbs in *-iter: fort<u>iter</u>, brev<u>iter</u>, turp<u>iter</u>.* Examples: *Pulchrē et rēctē scrībis; Nec sōlum prāvē et turp<u>iter</u>, sed etiam nimis lev<u>iter</u> scrībis; Magister brev<u>iter</u> respondet* (ll. 69, 105–106, 134).

adverb

adjective	adverb
-us -a -um	*-ē*
-is -e	*-iter*

Some adverbs, e.g. *certē*, modify a whole phrase, like *<u>Certē</u> pulcherrimae sunt litterae Sextī* (l. 73). Others may belong to an adjective, like *aequē* in the teacher's remark to the two boys: *"Litterae vestrae <u>aequē foedae</u> sunt"* (l. 78).

The teacher goes on: *"Tū, Tite, neque pulchr<u>ius</u> neque foed<u>ius</u> scrībis quam Mārcus"*, and Titus retorts: *"At certē rēct<u>ius</u> scrībō quam Mārcus."* The examples show the <u>comparative of the adverb</u> ending in *-ius: pulchrius, foedius, rēctius* (i.e. the neuter of the comparative of the adjective used as an adverb). The teacher then exhorts: *"Comparā tē cum Sextō, quī rēct<u>issimē</u> et pulcherr<u>imē</u> scrībit."* The <u>superlative of the adverb</u> ending in *-issimē (-errimē)* is formed regularly from the superlative of the adjective.

adverb
comparative: *-ius*
superlative: *-issimē*
-(err)imē

<u>Numeral adverbs</u> are formed with *-iēs: quīnqu<u>iēs</u>* 5×, *sex<u>iēs</u>* 6×, *sept<u>iēs</u>* 7×, etc.; only the first four have special forms: *semel* 1×, *bis* 2×, *ter* 3×, *quater* 4×. From *quot* and *tot* are formed *quot<u>iēs</u>* and *tot<u>iēs</u>* (see ll. 118–126, 133, 134).

numeral adverbs: *-iēs* [×]
(question: *quotiēs?*)

The verb *facere* has no passive form, but *fierī* functions as the passive of *facere*: *Vōcālis est littera quae per sē syllabam <u>facere</u> potest... Sine vōcālī syllaba <u>fierī</u> nōn potest* (ll. 23–25). Compounds of *facere* ending in *-ficere*, e.g. *ef-ficere*, are used in the passive: *stilus ex ferrō efficitur* (= *fit*).

active: *facere*
facit, faciunt
passive: *fierī*
fit, fiunt

The conjunction *cum* may serve to introduce a sudden occurrence, as in this example: *Titus sīc incipit: "Magister! Mārcus bis..." – <u>cum</u> Mārcus stilum in partem corporis eius mollissimam premit!* (ll 128–129).

29

Chapter 19

Undisturbed by their noisy children Julius and Aemilia are walking up and down in the beautiful peristyle, which is adorned with statues of gods and goddesses.

Iuppiter Iov|is (= Zeus)

Among the names of the gods notice the name of the supreme god *Iuppiter Iov|is;* the stem is *Iov-* (meaning 'sky'), and the long nominative form is due to the addition of *pater* weakened to *-piter.* The Roman gods were identified with the Greek, e.g. *Iuppiter* with *Zeus,* his wife *Iūnō -ōnis* with *Hēra, Venus -eris,* the goddess of love, with *Aphrodītē,* and her son *Cupīdō -inis* ('desire') with *Eros.*

Iūnō -ōnis (= Hēra)
Venus -eris (=Aphrodītē)
Cupīdō -inis (= Eros)

irregular comparison:
magnus māior māximus
parvus minor minimus
bonus melior optimus
malus pēior pessimus
multī plūrēs plūrimī

Iuppiter has the honorific title *Optimus Māximus,* which is the superlative of *bonus* and *magnus.* The comparison of these adjectives and their opposites *malus* and *parvus* is quite irregular: see ll. 13–16, 25–30, 36–37. So is the comparison of *multī:* comp. *plūrēs,* sup. *plūrimī* (ll. 52, 54).

superlative + partitive
genitive

The superlative is often linked with a partitive genitive. Julius calls his wife *optimam omnium fēminārum* (l. 30). Venus is described as *pulcherrima omnium deārum* (l. 21) and Rome as *urbs māxima et pulcherrima tōtīus imperiī Rōmānī* (ll.57-58). Without such a genitive the superlative often denotes a very high degree (so-called absolute superlative): Julius and Aemilia

absolute superlative

address one another as *mea optima uxor!* and *mī optime vir!* (ll. 90, 94), and Julius, who sent *flōrēs pulcherrimōs* to Aemilia (l. 78), calls his former rival *vir pessimus* (l. 110; cf. ll. 107, 128, 129).

neque ūllus ('and no...')

As you know, *et* is not placed before *nōn;* nor is it placed before *nūllus:* instead of *'et nūllus'* we find *neque ūllus* (see ll. 14, 24, 27). The pronoun *ūll|us -a -um* ('any') is declined like *nūll|us:* genitive *-īus* and dative *-ī* in the singular; *tōt|us, sōl|us* and *ūn|us* are declined in the same way (see ll. 32, 58).

nūllus, ūllus, tōtus, sōlus,
ūnus: gen. *-īus,* dat. *-ī*

genitive of description:
puer septem annōrum

How old are the children? *Mārcus octō annōs habet; Quīntus est puer septem annōrum* (l. 33). Such a genitive, which serves to describe the quality of a noun, is called 'genitive of description' (Latin *genetīvus quālitātis*). Of young Julius we are told: *adulēscēns vīgintī duōrum annōrum erat* (l. 40).

The last example has *erat,* not *est,* because this was ten years ago (he is no longer *adulēscēns*). Thus, by taking you back in time we teach you the verb form used when things of the past are described. Compare the two sentences *Nunc Iūlius Aemiliam amat* and *Tunc Iūlius Aemiliam amābat.* The form *amā|bat* is the past tense or preterite (Latin *tempus praeteritum*) of the verb *amā|re,* as distinct from *ama|t,* which is the present tense (Latin *tempus praesēns*). The preterite or past tense occurring in this chapter denotes a past state of things or an action going on (not completed) or repeated; this preterite is called the imperfect (Latin *praeteritum imperfectum,* 'uncompleted past').

past tense or preterite
present and past tense

imperfect
active
sing. 1. *-(ē)ba|m*
　　2. *-(ē)bā|s*
　　3. *-(ē)ba|t*
plur. 1. *-(ē)bā|mus*
　　2. *-(ē)bā|tis*
　　3. *-(ē)ba|nt*
passive
sing. 1. *-(ē)ba|r*
　　2. *-(ē)bā|ris*
　　3. *-(ē)bā|tur*
plur. 1. *-(ē)bā|mur*
　　2. *-(ē)bā|minī*
　　3. *-(ē)ba|ntur*

In the 3rd person the imperfect ends in *-ba|t* in the singular and *-ba|nt* in the plural; the consonant- and *ī*-stems have *-ēba|t* and *-ēba|nt:* *Iūlius et Aemilia Rōmae habitābant; Iūlius cotīdiē epistulās ad Aemiliam scrībēbat; Iūlius male dormiēbat.* During the couple's talk of their early love the 1st and 2nd persons are turned to account, as when Julius says: *"tunc ego tē amābam, tū mē nōn amābās..."* (l. 98); *"Neque epistulās, quās cotīdiē tibi scrībēbam, legēbās"* (ll. 101-102). The plural forms end in *-mus* and *-tis* preceded by *-bā-* or *-ēbā-,* e.g. *(nōs) amābāmus, (vōs) amābātis* (see ll. 124–127).

The imperfect is formed by inserting *-bā-* (1st and 2nd conjugations) or *-ēbā-* (3rd and 4th conjugations) between the stem and the personal endings: in the active *-m, -mus* (1st pers.), *-s, -tis* (2nd pers.) and *-t, -nt* (3rd pers.); and in the passive *-r, -mur* (1st pers.), *-ris, -minī* (2nd pers.) and *-tur, -ntur* (3rd

30

pers.). Note that the 1st person ends in *-m* and *-r* (not *-ō* and *-or*) and that *ā* is shortened before *-m, -r, -t, -nt* and *-ntur* (*amā|ba̯|m, amā|ba̯|r*, etc.). In the GRAMMATICA LATINA section you will find examples of all the forms.

You have already met the 3rd person of the imperfect of the irregular verb *esse: era|t, era|nt* (cap. 13). Now you learn the 1st and 2nd persons: *era|m, erā|mus* and *erā|s, erā|tis*. Compounds of *esse*, e.g. *ab-esse*, show the same forms: *ab-era|m, ab-erā|s*, etc., and so does *posse: pot-era|m, pot-erā|s*, etc.

imperfect of esse
sing.   plur.
1. *era|m*   *erā|mus*
2. *erā|s*   *erā|tis*
3. *era|t*   *era|nt*

The noun *domus -ūs* is a 4th declension feminine, but it has some 2nd declension endings: ablative singular *domō (in magnā domō)*, and in the plural accusative *domōs* and genitive *domōrum* (or *domuum*). The form *domī* (cap. 15, l. 81) is locative; for this form and acc. *domum* and abl. *domō* used as adverbs without a preposition, see the next chapter.

domus -ūs f., abl. *-ō*
pl. acc. *-ōs*, gen. *-ōrum*

In cap. 4 you learned that 2nd declension words in *-us* have a special form used when addressing a person, the <u>vocative</u>, ending in *-e*, e.g. *domine*. When Aemilia addresses her husband by name she uses the vocative *Iūlī:* "*Ō Iūlī!*" and she adds "*mī optime vir!*" (ll. 93-94). The vocative of personal names in *-ius*, e.g. *Iūlius, Cornēlius, Lūcius*, ends in *-ī* (a contraction of *-ie*): *Iūlī, Cornēlī, Lūcī*, and the vocative of *meus* is *mī*. Even *filius* has *-ī* in the vocative: Julius says "*Ō mī filī!*" to his son (cap. 21, l. 30).

personal names in *-ius*
and *filius:* voc. *-ī*
meus: voc. *mī*

The ending *-ās* in *māter familiās* and *pater familiās* (ll. 17, 38) is an old genitive ending of the 1st declension (= *-ae*).

Chapter 20

A happy event is in store for our Roman family. This gives the parents occasion for thoughts about the future, which in turn gives you a chance to get acquainted with the <u>future tense</u> (Latin *tempus futūrum*) of Latin verbs.

The first regular verbs to appear in the future tense are *ā-* and *ē-*stems (1st and 2nd conjugations) with the endings *-bit* and *-bunt* in the 3rd person, e.g. *habē|bit, habē|bunt; amā|bit, amā|bunt* (ll. 22–27). But when you come to consonant- and *ī*-stems (3rd and 4th conjugations) you find the future endings *-et, -ent*, e.g. *dīc|et, pōn|ent* and *dormi|et, dormi|ent* (ll. 32, 44-45). The corresponding passive endings are *-bitur, -buntur* and *-ētur, -entur* (ll. 28-29, 36). You also find examples of the future of *esse:* 3rd pers. sing. *erit*, plur. *erunt* (ll. 21, 23; even in compounds, e.g. l. 31 *pot-erit* of *posse*).

future
1st & 2nd conjugations
          active   passive
sing. 1. *-b|ō*   *-b|or*
      2. *-b|is*   *-b|eris*
      3. *-b|it*   *-b|itur*
plur. 1. *-b|imus* *-b|imur*
      2. *-b|itis* *-b|iminī*
      3. *-b|unt*   *-b|untur*

3rd & 4th conjugations
          active   passive
sing. 1. *-a|m*   *-a|r*
      2. *-ē|s*   *-ē|ris*
      3. *-e|t*   *-ē|tur*
plur. 1. *-ē|mus* *-ē|mur*
      2. *-ē|tis* *-ē|minī*
      3. *-e|nt*   *-e|ntur*

The 1st and 2nd persons of the future are put to use in the parents' conversation. You will find the endings (1) *-bō, -bimus* and *-bis, -bitis* added to *ā-* and *ē*-stems, e.g. *amā|bō, habē|bō*, etc., and (2) *-am, -ēmus* and *-ēs -ētis* added to consonant- and *ī*-stems, e.g. *discēd|am, discēd|ēs, dormi|am, dormi|ēmus*, etc. The passive endings are (1) *-bor, -bimur; -beris, -biminī*; (2) *-ar, -ēmur; -ēris, -ēminī*. The future of *esse:* 1st person *erō, erimus;* 2nd person *eris, eritis*.

esse
sing.   plur.
1. *erō*   *erimus*
2. *eris*   *eritis*
3. *erit*   *erunt*

The future is formed by the insertion between the stem and personal ending of (1) *-b-* in the 1st and 2nd conjugations, e.g. *amā|b|ō, habē|b|ō;* before the consonants in the endings *-s, -t, -mus, -tis, -nt, -ris, -tur, -minī, -ntur* a short vowel is inserted, mostly *-i- (amā|bi̯|s, amā|bi̯|t, amā|bi̯|mus*, etc.), but *-u-* before *-nt, -ntur (amā|bu̯|nt, amā|bu̯|ntur)* and *-e-* before *-ris (amā|be̯|ris);* even *ī|re* has *-b-* in the future tense: *(ab-, ad-, ex-, red-)ī|b|ō, ī|bi|s, ī|b|it*, etc. (ll. 131-132). (2) *-ē-* (but 1st pers. sing. *-a-*) in the 3rd and 4th conjugations, e.g. *dīc|a|m, dīc|ē|s*, etc.; *audi|a|m, audi|ē|s*, etc. (*-ē-* is shortened before *-t, -nt, -ntur*: *dīc|e̯|t, dīc|e̯|nt, dīc|e̯|ntur).*

31

You already know the 3rd person present of the irregular verb *velle: vult, volunt.* The 1st and 2nd persons are: *volō, volumus* and *vīs, vultis* respectively (ll. 55, 56, 64, 73). The negation *nōn* is not placed before *volō, volumus, volunt* and *velle;* instead we find the forms *nōlō, nōlumus, nōlunt* and *nōlle* (ll. 17, 55, 141, 157), which are contracted from *nē + volō* etc. The imperative *nōlī, nōlīte* is used with an infinitive to express a prohibition ('don't...!'), e.g. *"Nōlī abīre!"* (l. 69); *"nōlīte mē 'Iūliolam' vocāre!"* (l. 160).

domum acc. ('home')
domō abl. ('from home')
domī loc. ('at home')

The accusative and ablative of *domus, domum* and *domō,* are used without a preposition to express motion to or from one's home, e.g. *domum revertī* and *domō abīre* (see ll. 123, 137); the form *domī,* e.g. *domī manēre* (l. 127) is locative ('at home'). Cf. the rule applying to the names of towns: *Tūsculum, Tūsculō, Tūsculī. Domō,* like *Tusculō,* is the ablative of separation; so is the ablative with *carēre* ('be without', 'lack'), e.g. *cibō carēre* (l. 6; cf. *sine* + abl.: *sine cibō esse*).

The personal pronouns *nōs* and *vōs* become *nōbīs* and *vōbīs* in the ablative and dative: *ā vōbīs, ā nōbīs* (ll. 130, 136; dative: cap. 21, ll. 91, 109).

Chapter 21

The chapter opens with Marcus coming home from school. He seems to be in a bad way: he is wet and dirty, and his nose is bleeding. Whatever can have happened on his way home? This is what you find out reading the chapter. You are reading Marcus's version of the story, and whether it is true or not, you can use it to learn the verb forms that are used when you talk about an event that has taken place.

First of all you find the form *ambulāvit* of the verb *ambulāre* in the explanation given for the wet clothes: *Mārcus per imbrem ambulāvit* (l. 7). This tense is called the <u>perfect</u>, in Latin *tempus praeteritum perfectum,* 'past completed', as distinct from the <u>imperfect</u> tense or *praeteritum imperfectum,* 'past not completed'. The difference is that the imperfect, as we know, describes a state of affairs or an ongoing or repeated (habitual) action in the past, while the perfect tense tells about what once happened and is now finished. Compare the two preterites in the sentences: *Iūlia cantābat... Tum Mārcus eam pulsāvit!* The perfect often occurs in connection with the present tense, when the present result of a past action is described ('the present perfect'), e.g. *Iam Iūlia plōrat, quia Mārcus eam pulsāvit* (English 'has hit').

perfect
personal endings
sing. plur.
1. *-ī* *-imus*
2. *-istī* *-istis*
3. *-it* *-ērunt*

The plural of *ambulāv|it* and *pulsāv|it* is *ambulāv|ērunt* and *pulsāv|ērunt: Puerī per imbrem ambulāvērunt; Mārcus et Titus Sextum pulsāvērunt* (l. 13). The 3rd person perfect ends in *-it* in the singular and *-ērunt* in the plural. You find the same personal endings in the perfect forms *iacu|it* and *iacu|-ērunt* of *iacēre* (ll. 20, 21) and *audīv|it* and *audīv|ērunt* of *audīre* (ll. 23, 26). The endings of the 1st and 2nd persons, too, are different from the ones you know from the other tenses, as appears from this conversation between father and son (ll. 40–43): *Mārcus: "...ego illum pulsāvī!" Iūlius: "Tūne sōlus ūnum pulsāvistī?" Mārcus: "Ego et Titus eum pulsāvimus." Iūlius: "Quid? Vōs duo ūnum pulsāvistis?"* As you see, the 1st person has the endings *-ī, -imus (pulsāv|ī, pulsāv|imus)* and the 2nd *-istī, -istis (pulsāv|istī, pulsāv|istis)* in the singular and plural respectively. The parallel forms of *iacēre* are *iacu|ī, iacu|imus* (1st pers.) and *iacu|istī, iacu|istis* (2nd pers.), and of *audīre: audīv|ī, audīv|imus* (1st pers.) and *audīv|istī, audīv|istis* (2nd pers.).

32

As shown by the examples, the personal endings of the perfect are not added directly to the verbal stems *pulsā-, iacē-* and *audī-*, but to the expanded or changed stems *pulsāv-, iacu-* and *audīv-*. The consonant-stems undergo even greater changes in the perfect tense: thus the perfect of *scrībere* is *scrīps|it* and of *dīc|ere dīx|it* (ll. 113, 124), the stems being changed to *scrīps-* and *dīx-*. This special form of the verbal stem, to which are added the personal endings of the perfect, is called the <u>perfect stem</u>, whereas the basic stem of the verb is called its <u>present stem</u>.

	present stem	perfect stem
1.	pulsā-	pulsāv-
2.	iacē-	iacu-
3.	scrīb-	scrīps-
4.	audī-	audīv-

From present stems ending in *ā* or *ī* (1st and 4th conjugations) perfect stems are regularly formed by the addition of *v*, e.g. *pulsā-: pulsā<u>v</u>-, audī-: audī<u>v</u>-*, and from present stems in *-ē* (2nd conjugation) by changing *ē* to *u: iacē-: iac<u>u</u>-*. The perfect stem of 3rd conjugation verbs (with present stems ending in a consonant) is formed in various ways, e.g. by adding *s* to the present stem. In *scrīb-: scrīps-* voiced *b* changes to voiceless *p*, in *dīc-: dī<u>x</u>-* only the spelling changes (*x = cs*). The verb *esse* has a separate perfect stem *fu-: fu|ī, fu|istī, fu|it*, etc. (see ll. 83–86, 105, 106).

scrīps- < scrībs-
dīx- < dīcs-

perf. stem of *esse: fu-*

In cap. 11 the doctor's remark *"Puer dormit"* was reported: *Medicus 'puerum dormīre' dīcit*, i.e. in the accusative and infinitive (acc. + inf.). *Dormi|t* is the present tense and the corresponding infinitive *dormī|re* is called the <u>present infinitive</u> (Latin *īnfīnītīvus praesentis*). In this chapter Julius says: *"Mārcus dormīvit"* and this remark is rendered in the acc. + inf.: *Iūlius 'Mārcum dormīvisse' dīcit* (l. 97). *Dormīv|it* is the perfect tense and the corresponding infinitive *dormīv|isse* is called the <u>perfect infinitive</u> (Latin *īnfīnītīvus perfectī*); it is formed by the addition of *-isse* to the perfect stem. Other examples are *intrāv|isse, iacu|isse, fu|isse: Iūlius 'Mārcum intrāvisse' dīcit, at nōn dīcit 'eum... humī iacuisse'; Mārcus dīcit 'sē bonum puerum fuisse'* (ll.73-74, 85).

<u>present infinitive</u>: *-re*

<u>perfect infinitive</u>: *-isse*

The sentence *Sextus Mārcum pulsāvit* becomes *Mārcus ā Sextō pulsātus est* in the passive (l. 11). The form *pulsātus -a -um*, an adjective of the 1st/2nd declension, is called the <u>perfect participle</u> (Latin *participium perfectī*). This participle is regularly formed by adding *t* to the present stem, followed by the various adjective endings *-us -a -um* etc., e.g. *laudāt|us -a -um, audīt|us -a -um, scrīpt|us -a -um* (here, too, change from *b* to *p*). In combination with the present of *esse* (*sum, es, est*, etc.) the perfect participle is used to form the <u>passive of the perfect</u>, as in the above example; the ending of the participle then agrees with the subject, e.g. *Iūlia ā Mārcō pulsāt<u>a</u> est; puerī laudāt<u>ī</u> sunt; litterae ā Sextō scrīpt<u>ae</u> sunt.* When combined with the infinitive *esse* the perfect participle forms the <u>perfect infinitive passive</u>, e.g. *laudātum esse: Mārcus 'sē ā magistrō laudāt<u>um</u> esse' dīcit* (in the acc. + inf. the participle agrees with the subject accusative, cf. *Aemilia... litter<u>ās</u> ā Mārcō scrīpt<u>ās</u> esse crēdit*, l. 122). The perfect participle is also used as an attributive adjective: *puer laudātus* (= *puer quī laudātus est*). It is passive in meaning, as opposed to the <u>present participle</u> in *-ns*, which is active.

perfect participle
-t|us -a -um

perfect passive
1.	*-t|us -a*	sum
2.		es
3.	...*um*	est
1.	*-t|ī -ae*	sumus
2.		estis
3.	...*-a*	sunt

perf. inf. passive
laudāt|um esse
-t|us -a -um -am | esse
-ī -ae -ōs -ās |

The nouns *cornū -ūs* and *genū -ūs* are <u>4th declension neuters</u> (acc. = nom., plur. *-a: cornu<u>a</u>, genu<u>a</u>*). See the paradigm in the margin of page 164.

4th declension neuter
cornū -ūs, pl. *-ua -uum*

Ali-quis -quid is an <u>indefinite pronoun</u>, which is used about an undetermined person or thing (ll. 65, 91; English 'someone', 'something').

<u>indefinite</u> pronoun
ali-quis ali-quid

The neuter plural of adjectives and pronouns is often used as a noun (substantively) in a general sense, e.g. *multa* (l. 90, 'a great deal'), *omni<u>a</u>* (l. 95, 'everything'), *h<u>ae</u>c* (l. 123, 'this'), etc. (= *et cēter<u>a</u>*).

With the verb *crēdere* the person whom you trust or whose words you believe is put in the dative: *"Mihi crēde!"* (l. 119; cf. ll. 140, 146).

crēdere + dative

33

Chapter 22

The picture over the chapter represents an ancient mosaic found inside the front door of a house in *Pompēiī*. The picture and the warning inscription *Cavē canem!* are evidence of the way the Romans tried to safeguard their houses against intruders. Every house was guarded by a doorkeeper (*ōstiā-rius* or *iānitor*), who had often a watchdog to help him.

So it is not easy for a stranger to be admitted to Julius's villa. First he must wake the doorkeeper and then he has to convince him that his intentions are not hostile. In this chapter the letter-carrier *(tabellārius)* tries to do this with the words: *"Ego nōn veniō vīllam oppugnātum sīcut hostis, nec pecūniam postulātum veniō"* (ll. 33-34). *Oppugnātum* and *postulātum* are the first

1st supine: *-tum*

examples of a verb form called supine (Latin *supīnum*), which is found with verbs of motion, e.g. *īre* and *venīre*, to express purpose. Other examples are *salūtātum venīre, dormītum īre, ambulātum exīre, lavātum īre* (see ll. 49–54).

Before the messenger reveals his intricate name *Tlēpolemus,* he says: *"Nōmen meum nōn est facile dictū"*(l. 43) and the doorkeeper, who has trouble catching the name, says: *"Vōx tua difficilis est audītū"* (l. 46). The forms *dictū* and

2nd supine: *-tū*

audītū are called the second supine – as distinct from the forms in *-tum,* the first supine. The 2nd supine is a rare form used to qualify certain adjectives, particularly *facilis* and *difficilis;* the above example, where the subject is *vōx,* could be paraphrased like this: *Difficile est vōcem tuam audīre.*

The supine endings *-um* and *-ū* are added to a modified stem-form, the so-

the supine stem

called supine stem, which is also used to form the perfect participle – and the future participle, as you learn in the next chapter. The supine stem is regularly formed by the addition of *t* to the present stem, e.g. *salūtā-: salūtāt-; audī-: audīt-; dīc-: dict-;* in *ē*-stems *ē* is changed to *i,* e.g. *terrē-: territ-;* and there are several other irregularities, especially in 3rd conjugation verbs, where the addition of *t* may cause changes by assimilation, e.g. *scrīb-: scrīpt-* (*p* is voiceless like *t*), *claud-: claus-* (*dt* > *tt* > *ss* > *s*).

verbal stems
1. the present stem [–]
2. the perfect stem [~]
3. the supine stem [≈]

When you know the three verbal stems, (1) the present stem, (2) the perfect stem, and (3) the supine stem, you can derive all forms of the verb from them. Consequently, to be able to conjugate (i.e. inflect) a Latin verb it is sufficient to know three forms, or 'principal parts', in which these stems are contained. Most useful are the three infinitives:

principal parts
1. pres. inf.
2. perf. inf. act.
3. perf. inf. pass.

   1. The present infinitive active, e.g. *scrīb|ere*
   2. The perfect infinitive active, e.g. *scrīps|isse*
   3. The perfect infinitive passive, e.g. *scrīpt|um esse*

These are the forms of irregular verbs that will be given in the margin when-ever needed (the 3rd form will be without *esse,* or missing if the verb has no passive, e.g. *posse potuisse;* of irregular deponent verbs you will find the passive present and perfect infinitives, e.g. *loquī locūtum esse*). The forms show various stem mutations, e.g. vowel lengthening *(emere ēmisse ēmptum; venīre vēnisse);* loss of *n* and *m (scindere scidisse scissum, rumpere rūpisse ruptum);* reduplication (doubling) of syllables in the perfect *(pellere pepu-lisse pulsum);* occasionally an unchanged perfect stem *(solvere solvisse*

symbols:
[~] perfect stem
[≈] supine stem

solūtum). To learn such irregularities a new exercise is now introduced in PENSVM A, where the missing perfect and supine stems are to be inserted in the verbs listed. – Symbols used: [~] for perfect stem and [≈] for supine stem.

quis quid indef. pron.
after *sī* & *num*

In the sentence *Sī quis vīllam intrāre vult...* (l. 7) the pronoun *quis* is not interrogative, but indefinite (= *aliquis*); the question *Num quis hīc est?* (ll. 27-28) does not ask 'who' is there, but whether 'anyone' is there, just as *quid* in the question *Num quid tēcum fers?* (l. 105) means 'anything' or 'something'. After *sī* and *num* the pronoun *quis quid* is indefinite (= *aliquis aliquid*).

sī quis/quid...
num quis/quid...?

The demonstrative pronoun *iste -a -ud* (declined like *ille -a -ud*) refers to something connected with the person addressed (2nd person): Tlepolemus says *iste canis* about the doorkeeper's dog (l. 86, 'that dog of yours') and talking about Tlepolemus's cloak the doorkeeper says *istud pallium* (l. 103).

demonstrative pron.
iste -a -ud

Compare the sentences *Iānitōre dormiente, canis vigilāns iānuam cūstōdit* (l. 23) and *Cane vīnctō, tabellārius intrat* (l. 119). *Iānitōre dormiente* is the ablative absolute with the present participle, which expresses what is happening now, i.e. at the same time (= *dum iānitor dormit...*, 'while...'). *Cane vīnctō* is the ablative absolute with the perfect participle, which expresses what has been done (= *postquam canis vīnctus est...*, 'after...').

ablative absolute +
(1) pres. part. (act.)0
/2) perf. part. (pass.)

Chapter 23

You will remember that at the end of cap. 18 the angry schoolmaster wrote a letter to Marcus's father. In this chapter you find out what is in that letter. The reproduction heading the chapter shows the kind of handwriting the ancient Romans used. Compare this with the text on page 180, and you will have no difficulty in deciphering the script.

Julius has to answer the letter. So after putting Marcus in his place, he says, *"Iam epistulam scrīptūrus sum"* (l. 125). He could have said, *"Iam epistulam scrībam"* using the ordinary future tense *scrībam*, for *scrīptūrus sum* is merely an extended form of the future which serves to express what someone intends to do or is on the point of doing; it is composed of the present of *esse* and *scrīptūrus*, which is the future participle (Latin *participium futūrī*) of *scrībere*. This participle is formed by adding ≈*ūr|us -a -um* to the supine stem, e.g. *pugnāt|ūr|us, pārit|ūr|us, dormīt|ūr|us* from *pugnāre, pārēre, dormīre*. You see these participles utilized when Marcus promises to turn over a new leaf (ll. 85–87). The future participle of *esse* is *futūr|us*, a form you know already from the expression *tempus futūrum*.

future participle
≈*ūr|us -a -um*

futūr|us -a -um

Julius's remark *"Epistulam scrīptūrus sum"* is rendered in acc. + inf.: *Iūlius dīcit 'sē epistulam scrīptūrum esse.'* *Scrīptūrum esse* is the future infinitive (*īnfīnītīvus futūrī*), which is composed of the future participle and *esse*. Other examples are *futūrum esse, pāritūrum esse, pugnātūrum esse, dormītūrum esse:* see the report of Marcus's promises ll. 90–92.

future infinitive
≈*ūr|um/-am/-ōs/-ās/-a*
esse

When Julius gets up to go, Aemilia suspects mischief and asks, *"Mārcumne verberātum īs?"* (ll. 113-114) using the supine with *īre* to express purpose. Her misgivings could be expressed in the acc. + inf.: *Aemilia Iūlium Mārcum verberātum īre putat,* but to avoid the ambiguity of two accusatives the passive form is preferred: *Aemilia Mārcum ā Iūliō verberātum īrī putat* (l. 114). The combination *verberātum īrī,* i.e. the supine + the passive infinitive *īrī* of *īre,* functions as future infinitive passive. Other examples are: *Ego eum nec mūtātum esse nec posthāc mūtātum īrī crēdō* (l. 118), and: *Dīc eī 'respōnsum meum crās ā Mārcō trāditum īrī'* (l. 133).

future infinitive passive
≈*um īrī* (supine + *īrī*)

When Marcus has been caught cheating, his father says, *"Nōnne tē pudet hoc fēcisse?"* (l. 79). The impersonal verb *pudet* tells that a feeling of shame affects one; the person affected is in the accusative, e.g. *mē pudet* (= *mihi pudor est,* 'I feel ashamed'). The cause of the feeling of shame can be expressed by an infinitive, as above, or by a genitive, e.g. *Puerum pudet factī suī* (l. 82).

impersonal verb *pudet*
+ acc. (& inf./gen)

Irregular verbs: with vowel lengthening: *legere lēgisse lēctum; fugere fūgisse;* with vowel change: *facere fēcisse;* with different stems: *ferre tulisse lātum.* with reduplication: *dare dedisse* (cap. 24, l. 96); *trā-dere* and *per-dere* are compounds of *dare,* which explains the perfect *trā-didisse* and *per-didisse.*

The present participle of *īre* looks regular enough: *i|ēns,* but the declension is irregular: acc. *eunt|em,* gen. *eunt|is,* etc. So also compounds, e.g. *red-īre,* part. *red-iēns -eunt|is.* Examples in ll. 106-107.

Chapter 24

From his sickbed Quintus calls Syra and asks her to tell him what has been going on while he has been lying alone and felt left out of things. Syra readily gives him all the details of Marcus's return home and what had gone before.

pluperfect
active

sing.	plur.
1. ~era|m	~erā|mus
2. ~erā|s	~erā|tis
3. ~era|t	~era|nt

passive

1. ≈us ≈a	eram
2.	erās
3. ... ≈um	erat
1. ≈ī ≈ae	erāmus
2.	erātis
3. ... ≈a	erant

Through this report you learn the tense called pluperfect (Latin *tempus plūs-quamperfectum*). It is used to express that an action comes before some point in the past, i.e. that something had taken place. The first examples are *ambu-lāv|erat, iacu|erat, pulsāt|us erat* and *pugnāv|erant* (ll. 66–68): *Mārcus nōn modo ūmidus erat, quod per imbrem ambulāverat, sed etiam sordidus atque cruentus, quod humī iacuerat et ā Sextō pulsātus erat. Puerī enim in viā pugnāverant.*

In the active the pluperfect is formed by the insertion of -*erā*- (shortened -*era*-) between the perfect stem and the personal endings: 1st person ~*era|m,* ~*erā|mus,* 2nd ~*erā|s,* ~*erā|tis,* 3rd ~*era|t* ~*era|nt.* In the passive the pluperfect is composed of the perfect participle and the imperfect of *esse* (*eram, erās, erat,* etc.), e.g. *Mārcus ā Sextō pulsātus erat = Sextus Mārcum pulsā-verat.* In the GRAMMATICA LATINA section you find examples of all the forms of the four conjugations and of *esse* (*fu|era|m, fu|erā|s, fu|era|t,* etc.).

Of the reflexive pronoun the form *sē* is accusative and ablative, the dative is *sibi* (cf. *tibi, mihi*): *Puer 'pedem sibi dolēre' ait: "Valdē mihi dolet pēs"*(l. 24).

Deponent verbs like *cōnārī* and *mentīrī* are always passive in form (except for the present and future participles: *cōnāns, cōnātūrus* and *mentiēns, men-tītūrus*); examples of these verbs in the present are: *Quīntus surgere cōnātur* and *Mārcus mentītur,* and in the perfect: *Quīntus surgere cōnātus est* and *Mārcus mentītus est* ('has tried', 'has lied'). The perfect participles of the verbs *patī, loquī, verērī* and *fatērī* are *passus, locūtus, veritus* and *fassus,* as appears from the examples: *tergī dolōrēs passus est; saepe dē eā locūtus est; Tabellārius... canem veritus est; Mārcus... 'sē mentītum esse' fassus est* (ll. 47, 60, 88, 101). The last sentence shows an example of the perfect infinitive: *mentītum esse.* – The imperative of deponent verbs ending in -*re,* e.g. *"Cōnsōlāre mē, Syra!"* (l. 40, cf. ll. 28, 41, 44), is treated in cap. 25.

The conjunction *quam* ('than') is used in comparisons after the comparative, e.g. *Mārcus pigrior est quam Quīntus.* Instead of using *quam* it is possible to put the second term in the ablative: *Mārcus pigrior est Quīntō.* Examples of this ablative of comparison: ll. 30, 77, 90, 108, 116, 117.

"Quōmodo Mēdus... puellam Rōmānam nōscere potuit?" asks Quintus; Syra answers: *"Nesciō quōmodo, sed certō sciō eum aliquam fēminam nōvisse"* (ll. 57–60). The perfect *nōvisse* of *nōscere* ('get to know') has present force: 'be acquainted with', 'know'. Cf. *Canis tē nōvit, ignōrat illum* (l. 94).

Note the adverbs *subitō, certō, prīmō* (ll. 12, 59, 100) which, like *postrēmō* and *rārō,* have the ending -*ō* (*prīmō,* 'at first', cf. *prīmum,* adv. 'first').

Chapter 25

In this and the next chapter you read some well-known Greek myths. These thrilling stories have fascinated readers through the ages, and innumerable poets and artists have drawn inspiration from the narrative art of the Greeks.

The place-names mentioned in the story can be found on the map of Greece. Among the names of towns note the plural forms *Athēnae* and *Delphī;* accusative *Athēnās, Delphōs*, ablative *Athēnīs, Delphīs*. These two cases, as you know, serve to express motion to and from the town: Theseus goes *Athēnīs in Crētam* and later *ē Crētā Athēnās*. But the ablative of plural town names is also used as a locative, so that *Athēnīs* can also mean *in urbe Athēnīs: Thēseus Athēnīs vīvēbat* (l. 52). The rule about the use of the accusative, ablative and locative (= genitive/ablative) of names of towns also applies to the names of small islands, e.g. *Naxus:* acc. *Naxum = ad īnsulam Naxum,* abl. *Naxō = ab/ex īnsulā Naxō;* loc. *Naxī = in īnsulā Naxō* (ll. 99, 100, 132). – A new name can be presented with *nōmine* ('by name', abl. of respect), e.g. *parva īnsula nōmine Naxus; mōnstrum horribile, nōmine Mīnōtaurus* (l. 26).

Athēnae -ārum f. pl.
Delphī -ōrum m. pl.

Athēnīs loc. (= abl.)

The imperative of deponent verbs ends in *-re* in the singular and in *-minī* in the plural (cons.-stems *-ere* and *-iminī*). You have already seen examples of *-re* in cap. 24 (e.g. l. 28: *"Intuēre pedēs meōs, Syra!"*) and in this chapter Theseus says to Ariadne: *"Opperīre mē!"* and *"Et tū sequere mē! Proficīscere mēcum Athēnās!"* (ll.75, 95), and to his countrymen: *"Laetāminī, cīvēs meī! Intuēminī gladium meum cruentum! Sequiminī mē ad portum!"* (ll. 92-93).

deponent verbs
imperative
sing. *-re*
plur. *-minī*

Transitive verbs like *timēre* and *amāre* are generally used with an object in the accusative, e.g. *mortem timēre, patriam amāre*. The nouns derived from these verbs, *timor* and *amor,* can be combined with a genitive to denote what is the object of the fear or love, e.g. *timor mortis* and *amor patriae* (ll. 77, 86). Such a genitive is called an objective genitive. Other examples are *timor mōnstrōrum, expugnātiō urbis,* nex *Mīnōtaurī* and *cupiditās pecūniae* (ll. 22, 46, 88, 122), the nouns *expugnātiō* and *nex* being derived from the verbs *expugnāre* and *necāre,* while *cupiditās* is derived from the verb *cupere* through the adjective *cupidus* (= *cupiēns*), which can itself be combined with an objective genitive, e.g. *cupidus pecūniae* (= *quī pecūniam cupit,* cf. l. 46). Even a present participle like *amāns* can take an objective genitive when used as an adjective, e.g. *amāns patriae* (= *quī patriam amat,* l. 51). – The verb *oblīvīscī* takes a genitive as object: *oblīvīscere illīus virī!* (l. 126, cf. l. 128). When the object is a thing the accusative is also possible (ll. 118, 130).

objective genitive

cupidus + gen.

amāns + gen

oblīvīscī + gen.

You have seen several examples of the accusative and infinitive with the verb *iubēre:* an active infinitive, as in *pater fīlium tacēre iubet,* expresses what a person is to do, while a passive infinitive, like *dūcī* in *quī eum ... in labyrinthum dūcī iussit* (l. 59) expresses what is to be done to a person ('ordered him to be taken into the labyrinth'; cf. cap. 26, ll. 7-8). Like *iubēre* the verb *velle* can take the acc. + inf.: *Tē hīc manēre volō* ('I want you to...') and *Quam fābulam mē tibi nārrāre vīs?* (ll. 2–4).

acc. + inf. pass.
with *iubēre*
acc. + inf. with *velle*

The perfect participle of deponent verbs can be used with the subject of the sentence to express what a person has/had done or did: *haec locūta Ariadna...* (l. 74, 'having said/after saying this...'); *Thēseus fīlum Ariadnae secūtus...* (ll. 84-85, 'following...'); *Aegeus arbitrātus...* (l. 137, 'who believed...').

A relative pronoun after a period functions as a demonstrative pronoun referring to a word in the preceding sentence, e.g. *Thēseus... Athēnīs vīvēbat. Quī nūper Athēnās vēnerat* (ll. 52, = *Is...*; cf. ll. 34, 61, 142).

The forms *nāvigandum* and *fugiendum* (ll. 94, 97) will be taken up in cap. 26.

ad + *-ndum:* cap. 26

Chapter 26

The story of the boy Icarus, who soared up to the scorching sun only to be plunged into the sea as the sun melted the wax that fastened his wings, has always been admired as a beautiful poetic picture of the penalty for arrogance and rashness. Syra, too, uses the story to warn Quintus to be careful.

In the expression *parātus ad pugnam* the accusative of the noun, *pugnam*, is used after *ad*. If the noun is replaced by the corresponding verb, the infinitive *pugnāre* is not used, but the form *pugnandum: parātus ad pugnandum*. This form, characterized by *-nd-* added to the present stem, is a kind of verbal noun called gerund (Latin *gerundium,* cf. the English '-ing'-form). The gerund is a 2nd declension neuter, but the nominative is missing: the accusative ends in *-ndum* (*pugna|nd|um*), the genitive in *-ndī* (*pugna|nd|ī*), the dative and ablative in *-ndō* (*pugna|nd|ō*). In consonant- and *ī*-stems (3rd and 4th conjugations) a short *e* is inserted before *-nd-: ad vīv|end|um, ad audi|end|um.*

gerund
acc. *-ndum*
gen. *-ndī*
abl. *-ndō*

In this chapter you find several examples of the gerund in the different cases (except the dative, which is rarely used). The accusative is only found after *ad*, e.g. *ad nārrandum* (l. 10). The genitive occurs with nouns, e.g. *fīnem nārrandī facere* (l. 13; = *fīnem nārrātiōnis f.*); *cōnsilium fugiendī* (l. 56, = *cōnsilium fugae*); *haud difficilis est ars volandī* (l.72); *tempus dormiendī est* (l. 122, = *tempus est dormīre*); or as objective genitive with the adjectives *cupidus* and *studiōsus: cupidus audiendī, studiōsus volandī* (ll.18, 43; cf. l.108); with the ablative *causā* the genitive of the gerund denotes cause or purpose: *nōn sōlum dēlectandī causā, sed etiam monendī causā nārrātur fābula* (ll. 134-135). The ablative of the gerund is found after *in* and *dē: in volandō* (l. 80); *dē amandō* (l. 154); or alone as the ablative of means or cause: *puerī scrībere discunt scrībendō; fessus sum ambulandō* (l. 24; cf. ll. 129, 130).

-ndī causā

adjectives
m.   f.   n.
-er -(e)r|a -(e)r|um
-er -(e)r|is -(e)r|e

m./f./n.
-ns, gen. *-nt|is*
-x, gen. *-c|is*

Some adjectives have *-er* in the masculine nom. sing. without the usual endings *-us* and *-is*, e.g. *niger -gr|a -gr|um* and (with *-e-* retained) *miser -er|a -er|um, līber -er|a -er|um,* and *celer -er|is -er|e* (in other adjectives of the 3rd declension *-e-* is dropped, e.g. *ācer ācr|is ācr|e,* 'keen', cf. *December -br|is*). Such 3rd declension adjectives have three different forms in the nominative singular – whereas those in *-ns* and *-x,* like *prūdēns* and *audāx,* have only one: *vir/fēmina/cōnsilium prūdēns/audāx* (gen. *prūdent|is, audāc|is*). Adjectives in *-er* have *-errimus* in the superlative, e.g. *celerrimus.* Irregular superlatives are *summus* and *īnfimus* (ll. 77, 79) from *super(us) -era -erum* and *īnfer(us) -era -erum* (comparative *superior* and *īnferior*).

āēr āer|is, acc. *-a*
(= *-em*)

The noun *āēr* (3rd decl. m., gen. *āer|is*) is borrowed from the Greek and keeps its Greek ending *-a* in the acc. sing. *āer|a* (l. 22, = *āer|em*).

*neque ūllus -a -um
neque quisquam
neque quidquam
neque umquam*

Like *ūllus -a -um* the pronoun *quis-quam quid-quam* ('anyone', 'anything') is used in a negative context, so that *et* is not placed before *nēmō, nihil: neque quisquam* (l. 26, 'and no one'), *nec quidquam* (cap. 27, l. 106, 'and nothing'); similarly *et* is avoided before *numquam* by using *neque umquam* (cap. 23, l. 26, 'and never':). *Quidquam* is changed by assimilation to *quicquam.*

es|tō es|tōte (imp.)

Instead of the short imperative *es! es|te!* of *esse* the longer form in *-tō -tōte* is often preferred: *es|tō! es|tōte!* In other verbs this so-called future imperative is not very common (it will be treated in cap. 33).

vidērī
(+ dat.)

Vidērī, the passive of *vidēre,* is used (with nom.+ inf.) in the sense of 'seem (to be)', e.g. *īnsulae haud parvae sunt, quamquam parvae esse videntur* (l. 94). In this function a dative is often added, e.g. *Mēlos īnsula... nōn tam parva est quam tibi vidētur* (l. 95, = *quam tū putās;* cf. ll. 96-97, 125); *puer... sibi vidētur... volāre* (l. 144, = *sē volāre putat*).

38

Chapter 27

Julius is the owner of a large estate in the Alban Hills, *mōns Albānus,* near Tusculum and the Alban Lake, *lacus Albānus.* The running of the farm is left to tenant-farmers, *colōnī.* Julius follows their work with great interest when he is in residence in his Alban villa. Here we meet him walking in his fields and vineyards, questioning his men about the quality of the crops.

In addition to many new words, you learn important new verb forms in this chapter. Compare the sentences *Servus tacet et audit* and *Dominus imperat ut servus taceat et audiat.* The first sentence tells us what the slave actually does. In the second sentence we are told only what his master wants him to do; this is expressed by the verb forms *tace|at* and *audi|at,* which are called subjunctive (in Latin *coniūnctīvus*) – in contrast to *tace|t* and *audi|t,* which are called indicative (in Latin *indicātīvus*). *Taceat* and *audiat* are the present subjunctive (in Latin *coniūnctīvus praesentis*) of *tacēre* and *audīre.*

The present subjunctive is formed by inserting -*ā*- between the present stem and the personal endings (short -*a*- before -*m,* -*t,* -*nt,* -*r,* -*ntur*). This makes the following endings in the active: 1st person -*a|m,* -*ā|mus,* 2nd -*ā|s,* -*ā|tis,* 3rd -*a|t,* -*a|nt,* and in the passive: 1st person -*a|r,* -*ā|mur,* 2nd -*ā|ris,* -*ā|minī,* 3rd -*ā|tur,* -*a|ntur.* However, these endings are found only in the 2nd, 3rd and 4th conjugations. Verbs of the 1st conjugation, the *ā*-stems, which have -*ā*- in the present indicative, have -*ē*- (shortened -*e*-) before the personal endings in the present subjunctive: in the active: 1st person -*e|m,* -*ē|mus,* 2nd -*ē|s,* -*ē|tis,* 3rd -*e|t* -*e|nt;* and in the passive: 1st person -*e|r,* -*ē|mur,* 2nd -*ē|ris,* -*ē|minī,* 3rd -*ē|tur* -*e|ntur.* In the section GRAMMATICA LATINA you will find examples of verbs with all these endings and of the irregular present subjunctive of *esse:* 1st person *sim, sīmus,* 2nd *sīs, sītis,* 3rd *sit, sint.*

While the indicative is used to express that something does actually happen, the subjunctive expresses a desire or effort that something shall happen. Such an indirect command can be conveyed by verbs like *imperāre, postulāre, ōrāre, cūrāre, labōrāre, monēre, efficere, facere, cavēre.* These *verba postulandī et cūrandī* are often followed by object clauses introduced by *ut,* or, if they are negative, by *nē* (or *ut nē*) and the subjunctive. Examples will be found in the account of Julius's dealings with his men, e.g. *Dominus imperat ut colōnus accēdat* (l. 78); *vōs moneō ut industriē in vīneīs labōrētis* (l. 125-126); *Pāstōris officium est cūrāre nē ovēs aberrent nēve silvam petant* (l. 139-140). As appears from the last example the second of two negative clauses is introduced by *nē-ve,* i.e. *nē* with the attached conjunction -*ve,* which has the same value as *vel.* The negation *nē* is also used in *nē... quidem* (ll. 55, 86, 'not even').

When discussing the use of the farmers' tools *(īnstrūmentum),* the ablative of instrument is needed: *Frūmentum falce metitur. Quō īnstrūmentō serit agricola? Quī serit nūllō īnstrūmentō ūtitur* (ll. 18–20). This and the following examples *(Quī arat arātrō ūtitur...)* show that *ūtī* ('use') takes the ablative.

Instead of the regular plural *locī* of *locus* you find the neuter form *loca* -*ōrum* (l. 30) which is usual in the concrete sense ('places', 'region').

The prepositions *prae* and *prō* take the ablative; the basic meaning of both is 'before', from which other meanings are derived *(prae* ll. 63, 83, *prō* ll. 71, 72). – *Abs* for *ab* is found only before *tē: abs tē* (l. 80, = *ā tē*). – Note the ablative of separation (without *ab*) with *pellere* (*ut tē agrīs meīs pellant,* l. 89) and *prohibēre* (*Nōlī mē officiō meō prohibēre!* l. 174).

The shepherd runs after his sheep *quam celerrimē potest* (l. 177): *quam* + superlative *(potest)* denotes the highest possible degree: 'as quickly as possible'.

subjunctive
present
2nd, 3rd & 4th conj.

	active	passive
sg. 1.	-*a|m*	-*a|r*
2.	-*ā|s*	-*ā|ris*
3.	-*a|t*	-*ā|tur*
pl. 1..	-*ā|mus*	-*ā|mur*
2.	-*ā|tis*	-*ā|minī*
3.	-*a|nt*	-*a|ntur*

1st conj.

	active	passive
sg. 1.	-*e|m*	-*e|r*
2.	-*ē|s*	-*ē|ris*
3.	-*e|t*	-*ē|tur*
pl. 1.	-*ē|mus*	-*ē|mur*
2.	-*ē|tis*	-*ē|minī*
3.	-*e|nt*	-*e|ntur*

esse

	sing.	plur.
1.	*si|m*	*sī|mus*
2.	*sī|s*	*sī|tis*
3.	*si|t*	*si|nt*

indirect command
or request
verba postulandī et cūrandī: ut/nē + subj.

ūtī + abl.

locus -ī m., pl. *locī/loca -ōrum* m./n.

prae, prō + abl.

abs tē = ā tē

quam + sup. *(potest)*
('as... as possible')

39

Chapter 28

In this chapter and the next you hear more about Medus and Lydia. When the violent storm dies down, their ship sails on over the open sea. Lydia shows Medus the little book that she has brought with her and reads aloud from it, and in this way you become acquainted with the oldest Latin translation of the New Testament, used by St. Jerome in the 4th century in his Latin version of the Bible (the so-called Vulgate, *Vulgāta*, the 'popular' version).

Besides new examples of the present subjunctive after *verba postulandī et cūrandī* in the present tense, you now find the imperfect subjunctive after the same verbs in the past tense: *Iēsūs nōn sōlum faciēbat ut caecī vidērent, surdī audīrent, mūtī loquerentur, sed etiam verbīs efficiēbat ut mortuī surgerent et ambulārent* (ll. 34–37). The imperfect subjunctive is formed by inserting *-rē-*, in consonant-stems *-erē-*, between the present stem and the personal endings (short *e* before *-m, -t, -nt, -r, -ntur*), e.g. *vidē|re|m, vidē|rē|s, vidē|re|t*, etc., and *surg|ere|m, surg|erē|s, surg|ere|t*, etc. The imperfect subjunctive of *esse* is *esse|m, essē|s, esse|t*, etc. Examples of all the forms of the four conjugations active and passive and of *esse* are found in the section GRAMMATICA LATINA

While the present subjunctive follows a main verb in the present, the imperfect subjunctive is used after a main verb in the past tense (perfect, imperfect or pluperfect). Compare the sentences *Magister mē monet ut taceam et audiam* and *Magister mē monēbat (/monuit/monuerat) ut tacērem et audīrem*.

In the example *praedōnēs... nāvēs persequuntur, ut mercēs et pecūniam rapiant nautāsque occīdant* (ll. 132–134) the *ut*-clause with the present subjunctives *rapiant* and *occīdant* expresses the purpose of the pursuit. Here again, the subjunctive denotes an action that is only intended, not actually accomplished. Other purpose clauses (final clauses), with the imperfect subjunctive because the main verb is in the past tense, are these: *Petrus ambulābat super aquam, ut venīret ad Iēsum* (l. 103) and *ē vīllā fūgī, ut verbera vītārem atque ut amīcam meam vidērem ac semper cum eā essem* (ll. 162-163). In English purpose is expressed by an infinitive preceded by 'to' or 'in order to'.

Num quis tam stultus est ut ista vēra esse crēdat? (ll. 90-91) is an example of another type of *ut*-clause with the subjunctive, a so-called result clause or consecutive clause (*ut... crēdat* tells the consequence of anyone being so stupid); cf. *ita ... ut Iuppiter rēx caelī esset* (l. 87). More examples in cap. 29.

Most Latin *ut*-clauses with the subjunctive correspond to English 'that'-clauses. But don't forget that *ut* is also a comparative conjunction (English 'like' or 'as'); in this function *ut* is followed by the indicative, e.g. *ut tempestās mare tranquillum turbāvit...* (ll. 8-9) and *ut spērō* (l. 149).

Note the difference between (1) *verba dīcendī et sentiendī*, which are combined with the acc. + inf., and (2) *verba postulandī et cūrandī*, which take an *ut*-clause in the subjunctive. Some verbs can have both functions, e.g. *persuādēre* in these two examples: *mihi nēmō persuādēbit hominem super mare ambulāre posse* (ll. 110-111), and *Mēdus mihi persuāsit ut sēcum venīrem* (ll. 174-175; English 'convince' and 'persuade'). In both senses *persuādēre* takes the dative (like *oboedīre, impendēre, servīre,* and *prōdesse, nocēre*).

In the last example note *sēcum* and compare: *Dāvus... eum sēcum venīre iubet* (cap. 14, l. 87 = *eī imperat ut sēcum veniat*); *Pāstor... dominum ōrat nē sē verberet* (cap. 27, l. 158); *Mēdus... eam... rogat ut aliquid sibi legat* (l. 57); *[Iaīrus] Iēsum rogāvit ut fīliam suam mortuam suscitāret* (l. 65-66). In *ut/nē*-clauses expressing an indirect command the reflexive pronouns *sē, sibi, suus* refer to the subject of the main verb, i.e. the person ordering, requesting, etc.

Margin notes

subjunctive
imperfect
active
sing. 1. *-(e)re|m*
    2. *-(e)re|s*
    3. *-(e)re|t*
plur. 1. *-(e)rē|mus*
    2. *-(e)rē|tis*
    3. *-(e)re|nt*
passive
sing. 1. *-(e)re|r*
    2. *-(e)rē|ris*
    3. *-(e)rē|tur*
plur. 1. *-(e)rē|mur*
    2. *-(e)rē|minī*
    3. *-(e)re|ntur*
esse
  sing.   plur.
1. *esse|m essē|mus*
2. *essē|s essē|tis*
3. *esse|t esse|nt*

purpose/final clause:
ut/nē + subjunctive
(*fīnālis -e* < *fīnis*, 'end',
'purpose')

result/consecutive clause:
ut + subjunctive
(*consecūtīvus -a -um*
< *cōnsequī*)

comparative clause:
ut + indicative

verba dīcendī et sentiendī + acc.+ inf.
verba postulandī et cūrandī + *ut/nē* + subj.

reflexive *sē, sibi, suus* in
indirect command

40

Chapter 29

The Roman merchant, who is ruined because his goods had to be thrown overboard during the storm, cannot fully share the joy of the others at being saved. He exclaims *"Heu, mē miserum!"* (acc. in exclamation) and asks in despair: *"Quid faciam? Quid spērem? Quōmodo uxōrem et līberōs alam?"* (ll. 22–24); *"quōmodo vīvāmus sine pecūniā?"* (l. 51). In this kind of deliberative question, when you ask irresolutely what to do, the verb is in the subjunctive. A deliberative question can also be the object of a verb, e.g. *interrogāre, nescīre,* or *dubitāre: Vir ita perturbātus est ut sē interroget, utrum in mare saliat an in nāve remaneat* (ll. 57–59); *Mēdus rubēns nescit quid respondeat* (cap. 28, l. 184). But in such indirect questions the verb is in the subjunctive even when the direct question would have the indicative. In cap. 28 (l. 187) Lydia asked: *"nōnne tua erat ista pecūnia?"* now she says, *"Modo tē interrogāvī tuane esset pecūnia."* (ll. 127-128). The king's question to the sailors is rendered: *rēx eōs interrogāvit 'num scīrent ubi esset Ariōn et quid faceret.'* (ll. 105-106). Cf. *dubitō num haec fābula vēra sit* (ll. 116-117).

After the conjunction *cum* the verb is in the indicative in clauses describing something that happens usually or repeatedly, e.g. *Semper gaudeō, cum dē līberīs meīs cōgitō* (l. 47) and *tū numquam mē salūtābās, cum mē vidēbās* (cap. 19, l. 100). *Cum* in this function is called *'cum' iterātīvum* (from *iterāre,* 're-peat'). When the *cum*-clause indicates what once took place at the same time as something else, its verb is mostly in the imperfect subjunctive. The stories about *Arīōn* and *Polycratēs* contain several *cum*-clauses of this kind, e.g. *Cum Ariōn ex Italiā in Graeciam nāvigāret magnāsque dīvitiās sēcum habēret...* (ll. 78–80); *cum iam vītam dēspērāret, id ūnum ōrāvit...* (ll. 88-89); *Cum haec falsa nārrārent, Arīōn repente... appāruit* (l. 110); *Ānulum abiēcit, cum sēsē nimis fēlīcem esse cēnsēret* (ll. 156-157, cf. l. 171). The examples show that *cum* introduces both temporal and causal clauses (in English 'when' and 'as'); the latter can also have the verb in the present subjunctive, e.g. *Gubernātor, cum omnēs attentōs videat, hanc fābulam nārrat...* (l. 76).

Several of the *ut*-clauses with the subjunctive in this chapter are result clauses (preceded by *tam, tantus, ita*): ll. 58, 67, 68, 71, 86-87, 159-160. The example *piscem cēpit quī tam fōrmōsus erat ut piscātor eum nōn vēnderet* (ll. 167-168) shows that a result clause has the negation *nōn,* unlike purpose clauses, which have *nē* (= *ut nē*), e.g. *nē strepitū cantum eius turbārent* (l. 73).

In order to indicate how much you value something genitives like *magnī, parvī, plūris, minōris* can be added to *aestimāre* (or *facere* in the same sense). Examples: *Mercātōrēs mercēs suās magnī aestimant, vītam nautārum parvī aestimant* (ll. 6-7); *"Nōnne līberōs plūris aestimās quam mercēs istās?"* (l. 27). – With *accūsāre* the charge is in the genitive: *Lydia pergit eum fūrtī accūsāre* (l. 137). – A partitive genitive may qualify a pronoun, e.g. *aliquid pecūliī, nihil malī* (ll. 135, 157). The partitive genitive of *nōs, vōs* is *nostrum, vestrum: nēmō nostrum/vestrum* (ll. 39, 43). – Note *nōbīs-cum, vōbīs-cum* (ll. 40, 57) with the preposition *cum* attached as in *mē-, tē-, sē-cum* (cf. *quō-cum:* cap. 33, l. 154).

Many verbs are formed with prefixes, mostly prepositions. Examples in this chapter: *dē-terrēre, ā-mittere, in-vidēre, per-mittere, per-movēre, sub-īre, ex-pōnere, re-dūcere* (*re-* means 'back' or 'again'). Prefixes cause a short *a* or *e* in the verbal stem to be changed to *i*. Thus from *facere* is formed *af-, cōn-, ef-, per-ficere,* from *capere* *ac-, in-, re-cipere,* from *rapere* *ē-, sur-ripere,* from *salīre* *dē-silīre,* from *fatērī* *cōn-fitērī,* from *tenēre* *abs-, con-, re-tinēre,* from *premere* *im-primere.* Similarly *iacere* becomes *-iicere,* but the spelling *ii* is avoided by writing *-icere,* e.g. *ab-, ad-, ē-, prō-icere* (pronounce [*-yikere*]).

(marginal notes:)

deliberative question: *quid faciam?*

subjunctive in indirect questions

cum (iterātīvum) + indicative

cum + subjunctive

result clauses: *ut..., ut nōn...*

purpose clauses: *ut..., nē...*

genitive of value: *magnī, parvī plūris, minōris*

accūsāre + gen.

pronoun + partitive genitive

prefixes: *ab/ā-, ad-, con-, dē-, ex/ē-, in-, per-, prō-, re-, sub-,* etc.
facere > *-ficere*
capere > *-cipere*
rapere > *-ripere*
salīre > *-silīre*
tenēre > *-tinēre*
premere > *-primere*
iacere > *-icere*

41

Chapter 30

In this and the following chapter you read about a dinner-party in the home of Julius and Aemilia. The guests are good friends of the family. The dinner begins at the early hour of four o'clock in the afternoon (*hōra decima*), the normal time for the principal meal of the Romans. We hear about the arrangement of a typical Roman dining-room, the *triclīnium*, where the guests reclined on couches. Such a dining-room was not designed for large parties, for not more than three guests could lie on each of the three couches grouped around the little table.

distributive numerals
1 *singulī -ae -a*
2 *bīnī*
3 *ternī*
4 *quaternī*
5 *quīnī*
6 *sēnī*
10 *dēnī*

Note that for the purpose of indicating how many guests are reclining on each couch, Latin does not use the usual numerals *ūnus, duo, trēs,* but the numbers *singulī, bīnī, ternī: In singulīs lectīs aut singulī aut bīnī aut ternī convīvae accubāre solent* (ll. 74-75). These <u>distributive</u> numerals, which are adjectives of the 1st/2nd declension, are used when the same number applies to more than one person or thing, e.g. *bis bīna* (2×2) *sunt quattuor; bis terna* (2×3) *sunt sex. In vocābulīs 'mea' et 'tua' sunt ternae litterae et bīnae syllabae.* Distributive numerals all end in *-n|ī -ae -a,* except *singul|ī -ae -a.* More examples will be found in cap. 33.

hortatory subjunctive
-ēmus! -āmus!

When at last the servant announces that dinner is ready, Julius says: *"Triclīnium intrēmus!"* (l. 87) and at table he raises his glass with the words: *"Ergō bibāmus!"* (l. 120). The forms *intrēmus* and *bibāmus* are the present subjunctive (1st pers. plur.) of *intrāre* and *bibere;* accordingly they denote an action that is merely intended, in this case an exhortation ('let's...'). In the next chapter you will find further examples of this <u>hortatory</u> subjunctive (Latin *hortārī,* 'exhort').

future perfect
active
  sing.   plur.
1. *~er|ō* *~eri|mus*
2. *~eri|s* *~eri|tis*
3. *~eri|t* *~eri|nt*
passive

1. *≈us ≈a*	*erō*
2.	*eris*
3. *...≈um*	*erit*
1. *≈ī ≈ae*	*erimus*
2.	*eritis*
3. *...≈a*	*erunt*

To indicate that an action will not be completed till some point in the future, the <u>future perfect</u> is used (Latin *futūrum perfectum*). The first examples of this new tense are *parāverit* and *ōrnāverit: Cēnābimus cum prīmum cocus cēnam parāverit et servī triclīnium ōrnāverint* (ll. 82–84). In the active the future perfect consists of the perfect stem with the following endings: 1st person *~er|ō ~eri|mus,* 2nd *~eri|s ~eri|tis,* 3rd *~eri|t ~eri|nt.* The passive is composed of the perfect participle and the future of *esse* (*erō, eris, erit,* etc.), e.g. *Brevī cēna parāta et triclīnium ōrnātum erit* (ll. 84-85; cf. l. 14). This tense is especially common in conditional clauses (beginning with *sī...*) in cases where some future action must be completed before something else can take place, e.g. *Discipulus laudābitur, sī magistrō pāruerit.* Further examples of this use will be found in the section GRAMMATICA LATINA.

fruī + abl.

Like *ūtī ūsum esse* (see l. 38) the deponent verb *fruī* ('delight in', 'enjoy') takes the ablative: *ōtiō fruor* (l. 23, cf. ll. 35 and 59)

adj. *-āns -ēns*
adv. *-anter -enter*

3rd declension adjectives in *-ns,* e.g. *prūdēns -ent|is, dīligēns -ent|is, patiēns -entis, cōnstāns -ant|is,* form adverbs in *-nter* (contraction of *-ntiter*): *prūdenter, dīligenter, patienter, cōnstanter.* Examples: *"dīligenter cūrō ut colōnī agrōs meōs bene colant"* ... *"Prūdenter facis..."* (ll. 33–35); *"Patienter exspectā, dum servī lectōs sternunt"* (l. 82; cf. cap. 33, l. 120: *cōnstanter*).

sitis -is f., acc. *-im,* abl. *-ī*
vās vās|is n., plur. *vās|a*
  -ōrum

A pure *i*-stem is *sitis -is* f.: acc. *-im* (*sitim patī,* l. 55), abl. *-ī* (*sitī perīre,* l. 57). – The noun *vās vās|is* n. follows the 3rd declension in the singular, but the 2nd declension in the plural: *vās|a -ōrum* (l. 98: *ex vāsīs aureīs*).

Wine was not often drunk undiluted (*merum*), it was customary to mix one's wine with water. The Latin expression is *vīnum aquā (cum aquā) miscēre* or *aquam vīnō* (dat.) *miscēre* (see ll. 115, 132). Cf. *cibum sale aspergere* or *salem cibō* (dat.) *aspergere* (see ll. 109, 111).

42

Chapter 31

As the wine flows the conversation among the guests proceeds more freely. The room echoes with discussions, stories and the latest gossip. Orontes outdoes the others in talkativeness, and ends up by raising his glass crying: *"Vīvat fortissimus quisque! Vīvant omnēs fēminae amandae!"* (l. 172).

Note that here the present subjunctive forms *vīvat* and *vīvant* are used to express a <u>wish</u>. So also *valeat* and *pereat* in the two verses that Orontes recites before he goes under the table (l. 196; *per-eat* is the present subjunctive of *per-īre*). This use of the subjunctive is called <u>optative</u> (Latin *optātīvus* from *optāre*). It is closely related to the <u>hortatory</u> subjunctive, which is found not only in the 1st person plural (e.g. *"Gaudeāmus atque amēmus!"* l. 173), but also in the 3rd person, as in this exhortation by Orontes: *"Quisquis fēminās amat, pōculum tollat et bibat mēcum!"* (ll. 176-177).

optative subjunctive
hortatory subjunctive

Orontes's *vīvat* and *vīvant* apply first to *fortissimus quisque* (i.e. 'everyone according as he is the bravest', 'all the bravest men') and then to *omnēs fēminae amandae*. This is an example of a verb form called <u>gerundive</u> (Latin *gerundīvum*) which is formed like the gerund by adding *-nd-* or *-end-* to the present stem; but the gerundive is an <u>adjective</u> of the 1st/2nd declension (*ama|nd|us -a -um* < *amāre*) and serves to express what is to be done to a person or thing. Thus a charming woman may be described as *fēmina amanda*, a hardworking pupil as *discipulus laudandus* (< *laudāre*), and a good book as *liber legendus* (< *legere*). Most frequently the gerundive is used with some form of the verb *esse*, as in these examples: *Pater quī īnfantem suum exposuit ipse necandus est* (ll. 132-133); *Ille servus nōn pūniendus, sed potius laudandus fuit* (ll. 161-162); *Nunc merum bibendum est!* (l. 177). It is also possible to say simply *bibendum est!* without adding what is to be drunk; in the same way we find expressions like *tacendum est, dormiendum est*, which state in general terms what is to be done (see l. 178). With the gerundive, which is a passive form, the dative (not *ab* + abl.) is used to denote the <u>agent</u>, i.e. the person by whom the action is to be performed: *Quidquid dominus imperāvit servō faciendum est* (l. 159-160).

gerundive
-(e)nd|us -a -um

gerundive + dative
(agent)

We have seen relative pronouns without an antecedent, e.g. *quī spīrat vīvus est*; *quod Mārcus dīcit vērum nōn est*, where one might have expected *is quī...*, *id quod...* The meaning can be generalized by using the <u>indefinite relative pronouns</u> *quis-quis* and *quid-quid* ('whoever' and 'whatever'), e.g. *Quisquis amat valeat!* (l. 196); *Dabō tibi quidquid optāveris* (l. 29). (*Quidquid* is often changed to *quicquid* by assimilation.)

quis-quis 'whoever'
quid-quid 'whatever'

The defective verb *ōdisse* ('to hate') has no present stem, but the perfect has present force: *ōdī* ('I hate') is the opposite of *amō*; the two verbs are contrasted in *Servī dominum clēmentem amant, sevērum ōdērunt* (l. 94). Cf. *nōvisse*, perfect of *nōscere* ('get to know'), meaning 'know': *nōvī*, 'I know'.

ōd|isse ↔ *amāre*
ōd|ī ↔ *amō*
ōd|eram ↔ *amābam*
ōd|erō ↔ *amābō*

The preposition *cōram* ('in the presence of', 'before') takes the ablative: *cōram exercitū* (l. 122). So does *super* when used instead of *dē* in the sense 'about', 'concerning': *super Chrīstiānīs* (l. 147, cf. l. 200).

cōram prep. + abl.
super prep. + abl. = *dē*

The verb *audēre* is deponent in the perfect tense: *ausum esse* (l. 169: *ausus est*), but not in the present. Conversely, *revertī* is deponent in the present tense, but not in the perfect: *revertisse*. Such verbs are called <u>semideponent</u>.

semideponent verbs
audēre ausum esse
revertī revertisse

The inscription on page 259 is a <u>graffito</u> ('scratching' in Italian) which a lovesick youth has scratched on a wall in Pompeii. It will help you to decipher the characters when you know that the inscription contains the two verses quoted by Orontes (ll. 196-197, only the first syllable is missing).

Chapter 32

The fear of pirates gives rise to a long discussion on board the ship. Medus tells the story of the circumstances in which he was sent to prison and sold as a slave. This story mollifies Lydia, so when finally the danger is over, the two are once more on the best of terms.

During the discussion the merchant quotes two verses without giving the poet's name. The helmsman does not ask a direct question: *"Quī poēta ista scrīpsit?"* with the verb in the indicative, but uses an indirect question with the subjunctive: *"Nesciō quī poēta ista scrīpserit"* (l. 106). *Scrīps|erit* is the perfect subjunctive (Latin *coniūnctīvus perfectī*) of *scrībere*. This tense is formed in the active by inserting *-eri-* between the perfect stem and the personal endings: 1st person *~eri|m ~eri|mus*, 2nd *~eri|s ~eri|tis*, 3rd *~eri|t ~eri|nt* – i.e. the same endings as in the future perfect except for the 1st person singular *~erim* (where the future perfect has *~erō*). In the passive the perfect subjunctive is composed of the perfect participle and the present subjunctive of *esse* (*sim, sīs, sit,* etc.): *Iūlius dubitat num Mārcus ā magistrō laudātus sit* (= *num magister Mārcum laudāverit*).

The perfect subjunctive is used in indirect questions concerning completed actions, when the main verb is in the present tense, as in the above examples (cf. ll. 84, 132, 134, 155, 169, 216) – or in the (present) perfect (l. 82) or future (ll. 138-139). With *nē* the 2nd person of this tense expresses a prohibition: *nē timueris! nē timueritis!* (ll. 215, 199, = *nōlī/nōlīte timēre!*), cf. ll. 162, 182, 211.

The negation *nē* is also used with an optative subjunctive, e.g. *Utinam nē pīrātae mē... occīdant!* (l. 179-180). *Utinam* often introduces wishes, e.g. *Utinam aliquandō līber patriam videam!* (l. 157, cf. ll. 182-183, 223). An expression of fear that something may happen implies a wish that it may not happen; this is why verbs expressing fear, *timēre, metuere* and *verērī*, are followed by *nē* + subjunctive, e.g. *Timeō nē pīrātae mē occīdant* (cf. ll. 212-213; this *nē*-clause corresponds to an English 'that'-clause).

Like *oblīvīscī* its opposite *reminīscī* can take a genitive as object, e.g. *eius temporis reminīscor* (l. 155-156); so also *meminisse* (l. 126), a defective verb which, like *ōdisse*, has no present stem: the perfect form *meminī* ('I remember') is the opposite of *oblītus sum* ('I have forgotten').

The prefix *ali-* serves to make interrogative words indefinite. From *quot?* is made *ali-quot,* from *quandō? ali-quandō,* from *quantum? ali-quantum,* and from *quis? quid? ali-quis ali-quid.* However, *quis quid* is used (without *ali-*) as an indefinite pronoun after *sī* and *num* (see cap. 22) and after *nē*: *Nihil cuiquam nārrāvī dē eā rē, nē quis mē glōriōsum exīstimāret* (ll. 135-136).

The impersonal expressions *fit* and *accidit* may be followed by an *ut*-clause with the subjunctive telling what happens: *rārō fit ut nāvis praedōnum in marī Internō appāreat* (ll. 42-43); the *ut*-clause is the subject of *fit.*

The ablative in *tantā audāciā sunt* (l. 49) describes a quality and is called *ablātīvus quālitātis* or ablative of description; cf. *bonō animō esse* (cap. 29, ll. 122-123). – With *līberāre* we find the ablative of separation: *servitūte līberābantur* (l. 6). So also with *opus esse: Quid opus est armīs?* (l. 78; cf. ll. 118, 195).

The noun *vīs* ('strength', 'force', 'violence') has only three forms in the singular: nom. *vīs,* acc. *vim* (l. 13), and abl. *vī* (l. 77). The plural *vīrēs -ium* means physical strength: *nautae omnibus vīribus rēmigant* (l. 53, cf. l. 66).

After *mīlia* the partitive genitive is used, e.g. *duo mīlia annōrum.* Here *sēstertius* has the older short ending *-um* instead of *-ōrum: decem mīlia sēstertium* (l. 91, cf. l. 170).

Margin notes:

perfect subjunctive
active

sing.	plur.
1. *~eri|m*	*~eri|mus*
2. *~eri|s*	*~eri|tis*
3. *~eri|t*	*~eri|nt*

passive

1. *≈us ≈a*	*sim*
2.	*sīs*
3. *...≈um*	*sit*
1. *≈ī ≈ae*	*sīmus*
2.	*sītis*
3. *...≈a*	*sint*

nē ~eris! = *nōlī ~re!*
nē ~eritis! = *nōlīte ~re!*

utinam (nē) + subj.
(optative)

timēre nē + subj.

oblīvīscī, reminīscī, meminisse + gen.

ali-quis -quid, -quot, -quandō, -quantum

sī/num/nē quis/quid...

fit/accidit ut + subj.

ablātīvus quālitātis,
abl. of description

vīs, acc. *vim,* abl. *vī*
plur. *vīrēs -ium*

III mīlia sēstertium
(= *-ōrum*)

44

Chapter 33

The chapter consists mainly of a letter to Aemilia from her brother, who is in Germania on military service. From this letter you learn more military terms.

You also learn the last remaining Latin tense, the <u>pluperfect subjunctive</u> (Latin *coniūnctīvus plūsquamperfectī*). It is formed in the active by inserting *-isse-* (shortened *-isse-*) between the perfect stem and the personal endings: 1st person *~isse|m ~issē|mus*, 2nd *~issē|s ~issē|tis*, 3rd *~isse|t ~isse|nt*. The passive is composed of the perfect participle and the imperfect subjunctive of *esse* (*essem, essēs, esset*, etc.). The pluperfect subjunctive occurs in *cum*-clauses (where *cum* + pluperf. subj. = *postquam* + perf. ind.) and in indirect questions concerning completed action in the past, i.e. with the main verb in the preterite (imperfect, perfect or pluperfect). Examples: *Quī cum arma cēpissent et vāllum ascendissent* (= *postquam... cēpērunt/ascendērunt*), *prīmō mīrābantur quamobrem mediā nocte ē somnō excitātī essent... Ego quoque dubitāre coeperam num nūntius vērum dīxisset... Cum complūrēs hōrās ita fortissimē ā nostrīs... pugnātum esset* (ll. 109–121). – Note that in the <u>passive</u> an <u>intransitive</u> verb like *pugnāre* is <u>impersonal</u>, e.g. *ā Rōmānīs fortissimē pugnātum est* = *Rōmānī fortissimē pugnāvērunt* (cf. *nūntiātum est*, l. 105).

pluperfect subjunctive
active

	sing.	plur.
1.	*~isse|m*	*~issē|mus*
2.	*~issē|s*	*~issē|tis*
3.	*~isse|t*	*~isse|nt*

passive

1.	*≈us ≈a*	*essem*
2.		*essēs*
3.	*...≈um*	*esset*
1.	*≈ī ≈ae*	*essēmus*
2.		*essētis*
3.	*...≈a*	*essent*

cum + pluperf. subj. = *postquam* + perf. ind.

Aemilius's love of soldiering has cooled while he has been at the front. He wishes he <u>were</u> in Rome: *Utinam ego Rōmae essem!* (l. 67) using <u>optative subjunctive</u>; but in such an <u>unrealistic</u> wish that cannot be fulfilled the verb is not in the present, but in the <u>imperfect subjunctive</u>; cf. *Utinam hic amnis Tiberis esset et haec castra essent Rōma!* (ll. 70–71). The following sentences express a <u>condition</u> that can never be realized. *Sī Mercurius essem ālāsque habērem..., in Italiam volārem!* (ll. 73–75). Here, too, the imperfect subjunctive is used to express unreality; cf. ll. 82–85, 93–95. If such unrealistic wishes or conditions concern the past, the <u>pluperfect subjunctive</u> is used, as in Aemilius's final remarks: *Utinam patrem audīvissem...!* (l. 166) and *Sī iam tum hoc intellēxissem, certē patrem audīvissem nec ad bellum profectus essem* (ll. 181–182). More examples in ll. 163–164 and under GRAMMATICA LATINA.

imperf. & pluperf. subj. in unrealistic wishes and conditions

In the sentences *nūllum mihi ōtium est ad scrībendum* and *neglegēns sum in scrībendō* you see the <u>gerund</u> in the accusative after *ad* and in the ablative after *in*. Since the writing of letters is meant, it is natural to add the word *epistula*. The sentences then read: *nūllum mihi ōtium est ad epistulās scrībendās* and *neglegēns sum in epistulīs scrībendīs*. As you see, *ad* and *in* cause both the following words to be put in the accusative and ablative respectively, so that the verb form agrees with *epistulās* and *epistulīs*. In the same way *cupidus*, in the expression *cupidus patriae videndae* (l. 80), causes both the following words to be in the genitive, and *videndae* agrees with *patriae*. In this case, when the expression is not governed by a preposition, it is also possible to say *cupidus patriam videndī*, so that *cupidus* only affects the genitive *videndī*, a gerund which has the accusative *patriam* as its object. In the adjectival forms *scrībendās, scrībendīs, videndae* etc. we have a special application of the gerundive (so-called 'gerundive attraction'). Examples: *in epistulīs scrībendīs* (l. 94); *ad epistulam scrībendam* (ll. 97–98); *ad castra dēfendenda* (l. 116); *ad eōs persequendōs* (l. 132, = *ut eōs persequerentur*).

ad scrībendum
ad epistulās scrībendās
in scrībendō
in epistulīs scrībendīs
ars scrībendī
ars epistulārum scrībendārum (= *ars epistulās scrībendī*)

More distributive numerals are introduced: 10 *dēnī*, 4 *quaternī*, 5 *quīnī*, 6 *sēnī* (ll. 2–3). The distributive numerals are used with <u>pluralia tantum</u>, e.g. *bīna* (2) *castra*; *bīnae litterae* (= *duae epistulae*); but here 1 is *ūnī -ae -a* and 3 *trīnī -ae -a*, e.g. *ūnae litterae* (= *ūna epistula*), *trīnae litterae* (= *trēs epistulae*), see l. 91.

distributive numerals
+ pluralia tantum:
1 *ūnī|ī -ae -a*
3 *trīn|ī -ae -a*

Note the ablative of respect *numerō* in the expression *hostēs numerō superiōrēs* (l. 144, 'in number', 'numerically').

future imperative
    sing. plur.
1. 2. 4. *-tō* *-tōte*
3.   *-itō* *-itōte*

Aemilius ends his letter with some requests (ll. 187–189). Here he uses the so-called <u>future imperative</u> with the ending *-tō* (sing.), *-tōte* (plur.) added to the present stem, e.g. *nārrā|tō -tōte;* in consonant-stems *-i-* is inserted before the ending, e.g. *scrīb|itō -itōte* (but *es|tō, es|tōte* from *esse* and *fer|tō, fer|tōte* from *ferre*).

Chapter 34

By now you have advanced so far that you can begin to read Latin poetry. In this chapter you find poems by *Catullus* (c. 86–54 B.C.), Ovid (*Ovidius,* 43 B.C.–17 A.D.), and Martial (*Mārtiālis,* c. 40–104 A.D.). At the party Cornelius starts by quoting a line from Ovid's *Ars amātōria,* which makes Julius and Cornelius quote passages from a collection of love poems, *Amōrēs,* by the same poet. Julius goes on to read aloud some short poems by Catullus and a selection of Martial's witty and satirical epigrams (*epigrammata*).

free word order

When first reading the poems you will have to disregard the verse form and concentrate on the content. A major obstacle to understanding is the free word order, which often causes word groups to be separated. Here the inflectional endings will show you what words belong together; in some cases you will find marginal notes to help you, e.g. *ut ipsae spectentur* (l. 57), *nōbilium equōrum* (l. 62), *amor quem facis* (l. 65), *meae puellae dīxī* (l. 71); besides some supplementary (implied) words are given in italics. However, the important thing is to visualize the situation and enter into the poet's ideas. The comments made on the poems will be useful for this purpose

When you understand the meaning and content of the poems, it is time for you to study the structure of the verses, the so-called <u>meter</u>. This is explained in the GRAMMATICA LATINA section. The following is a summary of the rules:

syllable quantity:
a <u>short</u> syllable ends in
 a <u>short vowel</u>
a <u>long</u> syllable ends in
(1) a <u>long vowel</u>
(2) a <u>diphthong</u>
(3) a <u>consonant</u>
: any syllable that does
 <u>not</u> end in a short vowel
 is <u>long</u>
symbols:
long syllable: —
short syllable: ◡

The decisive factor in Latin verse structure is the length or <u>quantity</u> of the syllables. Syllables ending in a short vowel (*a, e, i, o, u, y*) are <u>short</u> and are to be pronounced twice as quickly as <u>long</u> syllables, i.e. syllables ending in a long vowel (*ā, ē, ī, ō, ū, ȳ*), a diphthong (*ae, oe, au, eu, ui*), or a consonant. In other words: <u>A syllable is short if it ends in a short vowel; all other syllables are long</u>. A long syllable is marked [—] and a short syllable [◡].

To define the meter each <u>verse</u> (*versus,* 'line') is treated like one long word:
(1) <u>A consonant at the end of a word is linked with a vowel (or *h*-) at the beginning of the next</u>. In a word like *satis,* therefore, the last syllable is short if the next word begins with a vowel or *h*-, e.g. in the combination *satis est,* where *-s* is linked with the following *e* in *est: sa-ti-s⌢est* – whereas the syllable *tis* is long in *satis nōn est: sa-tis-nō-n⌢est.*
(2) <u>A vowel (and *-am, -em, -im, -um*) at the end of a word is dropped before a vowel (or *h*-) beginning the next word</u>, e.g. *atque oculōs: atqu'oculōs; modo hūc: mod'hūc; passerem abstulistis: passer'abstulistis* (in *est* and *es* the *e* is dropped, e.g. *sōla est: sōla 'st; vērum est: vērum 'st; bella es: bella 's*). This is called <u>elision</u>, the vowel is said to be <u>elided</u> (Latin *ē-līdere,* 'eject').

elision

Each verse can be divided into a certain number of <u>feet</u> (Latin *pedēs*) composed of two or three syllables. The commonest feet are: the <u>trochee</u> (Latin *trochaeus*), consisting of one long and one short syllable [— ◡]; the <u>iamb</u> (Latin *iambus*), one short and one long [◡ —]; and the <u>dactyl</u> (Latin *dactylus*), one long and two short syllables [— ◡◡]. The two short syllables of the dactyl

metrical <u>feet</u>:
trochee — ◡
iamb ◡ —
dactyl — ◡◡
spondee — —

are often replaced by one long syllable, making a foot consisting of two long syllables [— —] which is called a <u>spondee</u> (Latin *spondēus*).

The favorite verse with Latin poets is the <u>hexameter</u>, which consists of six feet, the first five of which are dactyls or spondees – the fifth, however, is always a dactyl – and the sixth a spondee (or trochee):

— ⏑⏑| — ⏑⏑| — ⏑⏑| — ⏑⏑| — ⏑⏑| — ⏑̮

hexameter

The hexameter often alternates with the slightly shorter <u>pentameter</u>, which can be divided into two halves of 2½ feet, each conforming to the beginning of the hexameter (but there are no spondees in the second half):

— ⏑⏑| — ⏑⏑| — ‖ — ⏑⏑| — ⏑⏑| —

pentameter

The pentameter never stands alone, but always comes after a hexameter (in the text the pentameters are indented). Such a couplet, consisting of a hexameter and a pentameter, is called an <u>elegiac couplet</u>, because it was used in <u>elegies</u>, i.e. poems expressing personal sentiments, mainly love poems.

hexameter + penta-meter = elegiac couplet

Catullus frequently uses the <u>hendecasyllable</u> (Latin *versus hendecasyllabus*, 'eleven-syllable verse'), which consists of these eleven syllables:

— — — ⏑⏑ — ⏑ — ⏑ — ⏓

hendecasyllable

It can be divided into a spondee, a dactyl, two trochees and a spondee (or trochee). (Occasionally the first syllable is short.)

When Latin verse is read aloud, the rhythm is marked by the regular alternation of long and short syllables. Two short syllables are equivalent in length to one long. In modern European verse rhythm is marked by accent. Therefore modern readers of Latin verse are apt to put a certain accent on the first syllable of each foot. This may help you to get an idea of the verse rhythm, but do not forget that accent is of secondary importance in Latin verse, the important thing is the quantity of the syllables.

The Roman poets sometimes use the plural ('poetic plural') instead of the singular, especially forms in *-a* from neuters in *-um,* when they are in need of short syllables, e.g. *mea colla* (l. 75, for *meum collum*) and *post fāta* (l. 180, for *post fātum*). Like other authors a Roman poet may also use the 1st person plural *(nōs, nōbīs, noster)* about himself. You see this when Catullus calls his friend *venuste noster* (l. 152) and when Martial in his epigram on the response of the public to his books calls them *libellōs nostrōs* and concludes with the words *nunc nōbīs carmina nostra placen* (ll. 163, 166).

poetic plural

Martial, who himself writes poems *in inimīcōs,* says about the poet Cinna: *Versiculōs in mē nārrātur scrībere Cinna* (l. 172). Here *in* + accusative has 'hostile' meaning (= *contrā,* cf. the phrase *impetum facere in hostēs*). The passive *nārrātur,* like *dīcitur* (cap. 13, l. 52), is combined with the nom.+ inf.: *Cinna... scrībere nārrātur/dīcitur* = *Cinnam... scrībere nārrant/dīcunt.*

in + acc. = *contrā*

nom.+ inf. + *nārrātur*

Besides *imperāre* and *pārēre* you have met many other verbs which take the <u>dative</u>: *crēdere, nocēre, oboedīre, impendēre, servīre, (per)suādēre, invidēre, parcere, permittere, appropinquāre, placēre, (cōn)fīdere, ignōscere, resistere, minārī, studēre,* and several compounds with *-esse: prōd-esse, prae-esse, de-esse* ('fail') and *ad-esse* ('stand by', 'help'). In this chapter you find further examples: *favēre, nūbere, plaudere* (ll. 40, 126, 217). besides the impersonal verb *libet,* which – like *licet* – is usually combined with a dative: *mihi libet* (l.35, 'it pleases me', 'I feel like', 'I want'; cf. *mihi licet,* 'I may, I am allowed').

verbs + dative

A double *i (ii, iī)* is apt to be contracted into one long *ī,* as you have seen in the form *dī* for *diī.* When *h* disappears in *mihi* and *nihil,* we get the contracted forms *mī* and *nīl* (e.g. ll. 118 and 174). You also find *sapīstī* for

ī < *ii/iī*
mī < *mihi*
nīl < *nihil*

sapiistī (l. 190) – the latter form being a contraction of *sapīvistī:* the final *v* of the perfect stem tends to disappear, so that *-īvisse* becomes *-iisse/-īsse,* *-āvisse -āsse (-āvistī -āstī:* cap. 28, l. 106), *nōvisse nōsse* and *nōverat nōrat.* This form, the pluperfect of *nōscere,* comes to mean 'knew', e.g. *Ovidius...* *ingenium mulierum tam bene <u>nōverat</u> quam ipsae mulierēs* (l. 55); *suamque* <u>nōrat</u> *ipsam (: dominam) tam bene quam puella mātrem* (l. 93).

Chapter 35

Now that you have worked your way through all the declensions and conjugations of the Latin language, it is time to pause and take a comprehensive look at the grammatical system. To give you an opportunity to do this we present, in a slightly abbreviated form, a Latin grammar, the *Ars grammatica minor,* written by the Roman grammarian *Dōnātus* c. 350 A.D. This grammar is based on the works of earlier grammarians, rearranged in the form of question and answer, so it gives us an idea of the teaching methods used in antiquity – and much later, for the 'Donat' was a favourite schoolbook in Europe throughout the Middle Ages. Now it is up to you to show that you have learned enough to answer the questions on grammar put to schoolchildren in the Roman Empire. Apart from omissions, marked [...], the text of Donatus is unaltered (only in the examples on page 303 some infrequent words have been replaced by others).

The Latin grammatical terms are still in use. However, the <u>part of speech</u> (*pars ōrātiōnis*) which the Roman grammarians called *nōmina* is now divided into <u>nouns</u> (or <u>substantives</u>) and <u>adjectives</u>. The term *nōmen adiectīvum* dates from antiquity, but it was not till medieval times that the term *nōmen substantīvum* was coined (in English 'noun substantive' as opposed to 'noun adjective'). As a matter of fact, several of the Latin grammatical terms are adjectives which are generally used 'substantively' with a noun understood, e.g. *(cāsus) nōminātīvus, (numerus) plūrālis, (modus) imperātīvus, (gradus) comparātīvus, (genus) fēminīnum. Genus* is 'gender' in English; Donatus counts four genders, because he uses the term *genus commūne*

about words that may be both masculine and feminine, e.g. *sacerdōs -ōtis,* 'priest/priestess' (other examples: *cīvis, incola, īnfāns, testis, bōs, canis*).

The hexameter quoted by Donatus (l. 212) to illustrate the use of *super* with the ablative, is taken from the end of the first book of the 'Aeneid' (*Aenēis*), the famous poem in which Vergil (*Vergilius*) recounts the adventures of the Trojan hero Aeneas (*Aenēās*) during his flight from Troy (*Trōia*). Driven by a storm to Africa he is received in Carthage (*Carthāgō*) by Queen *Dīdō,* who questions him about the fate of the other Trojans, King Priam (*Priamus*) and his son Hector.

INDEX

(Numbers refer to pages)

A
ab/ā 15, 16; *abs* 39
ablative: prep.+ a. 9, 10, 15, 39, 43; absolute 27, 35; description 44; instrument 16, 18, 39; manner 20; price 18; comparison 36; difference 27; location 27; respect 21,37,45; separation 16,27,32,39,44; time 24; *ūtī, fruī* + abl. 39, 42
accent 5
accusative 13, 15; prep.+ a. 16, 17; extent 23; duration 24; exclamation 26, 41; a. + inf. 21, 33, 35, 37, 40; double a. 28
active 16
adjective 10, 48; 1st/2nd decl. 10, 22; 3rd decl. 22, 38; *-er* 22, 29, 38
adverb: *-ē -iter* 29; *-ō* 36; *-nter* 42; comparison 29; numeral adverbs (×) 29
age agite 15
agent: *ab*+abl. 16; dat. 43
ali- 44; *aliquis -quid* 33
alter, neuter, uterque 25
atque/ac 21
assimilation 19, 29, 34
aut/vel 24

C
calendar 23, 24
cardinals 24, 28
case 19
causā, -ndī c. 38
causal13, 20, 41
clause: causal 13,41; relative 13;; result 40, 41; purpose 40; conditional 42,45
coins 28
comparative 22; adv. 29
comparison 24, 30
compounds 17, 19, 41
conjugations 14
conjunction 11, 13, 19, 20
consonant 5; c.-stem 14 (vb.), 19, 21, 23
cum (conjunction) + ind. 20, 29, 41; + subj. 41, 45
cūr... quia 13

D
dare (short *a*) 28
dates 24
dative 17,18; interest 20,25; possessive 22; agent 43; verbs + d. 22, 33, 40, 47
declension: 1st-2nd 10, 19; 3rd 19, 20, 21; 4th 22, 33; 5th 23
defective verbs 25, 43, 44
deliberative subj. 41
demonstrative pronouns: *is* 15, 18; *hic ille* 17, 18; *ipse*

19; *īdem* 29; *iste* 35
deponent verbs: pres. 27; perf. 36, 37; imp. 37
diphthong 4
direct object 18; d. speech 21; d. question 41
distributive numerals 42, 45
domus 31; *-um -ō -ī* 31, 32
duo -ae -o 11, 25, 28

E
ecce 12
enumeration 12
et... et 17
esse est sunt 9, 17, 24, 26, 31, 33, 35, 38
ēsse ēst edunt 19, 20
ex/ē 17

F
feminine 11
ferre 23
ferī 27, 29; *fit ut...* 44
fractions 24
future 31; part., inf. 35
future perfect 42

G
gender 11, 19, 48
genitive 11; description 30; objective 37; partitive 12, 22,27,30,41,43; verbs + g. *accūsāre* 41, *oblīvīscī* 37, *reminīscī, meminisse* 44; *aestimāre* 41; *pudet* 36
gerund 38, 45
gerundive 43; g./gerund 45

H
hic haec hoc 17, 18
hortatory subj. 42, 43

I
īdem eadem idem 29
ille -a -ud 18
immō 17
imperative 14, 15, 17, 23; dep. 37; fut. 38, 46
imperfect 30, 32; subj. 40
imperfect/perfect 32
impersonal verb 20, 26, 35, 44, 45, 47
in + abl. 10,15, + acc. 17,47
indeclinable 11, 23, 28
indefinite pronouns 33, 34-35, 38, 44; i. rel. 43
indicative 14; i./subj. 39
indirect: i. command 39, 40; i. object 18; i. question 41; i. speech/statement 21
infinitive: pres. 20, 33; perf. 33; fut. 35
interrogative pronoun 13,18
intervocalic *-s-* > *-r-* 20, 21
intransitive verbs 13, pass. (impers.) 45
ipse -a -um 19
īre eō eunt 27, 31, 36

L
locative: *-ae -ī* 16; *-īs* 37; *domī* 31,32; *eō locō* 27
locus, plur. *locī/-a* 39

M
masculine 11, 27
meminisse (+ gen.) 44
mīlle 16; *mīlia* + gen. pl. 23, 27
multō + comp./ante/post 27

N
names 22
-ne...? 9
nē + subj. 39, 41, 44
negation 9, 13, 20, 39, 41, 44
nēmō 20
neque/nec 13, 21; *n. ... n.* 17; *n. ūllus/quisquam...* 30, 38
neuter 25
neuter: 2nd decl. 11; 3rd decl. 20, 21; 4th decl. 33; n. pl. *multa, omnia...* 33
nominative 13; n.+ inf.24,47
nōnne/num 17
noun, substantive, 10, 48
nōvisse 36, 43, 48
nūllus -a -um -īus 30
num 10; *num/nōnne* 17
numeral adverbs (×) 29
numerals 10, 11, 24, 28, 42

O
object 13, 18
objective gen. 37
ōdisse 43
omnis -e, omnēs -ia 25
optative subj. 43, 44, 45
ordinals 24, 28

P
participle: pres. 25, 33; perf. 33, dep. 37; fut. 35
passive 16, 33
past tense, preterite, 24, 30
paulō + comp./*ante/post* 27
perfect 32, 33; subj. 44
perfect/imperfect 32
perfect stem 33, 34
person 7; p. endings: act. 26, perf. 32; pass. 28
personal pronouns 13, 25, 26, 32; *mē-cum...* 25
pluperfect 36; subj. 45
plural 10, 15; poetic p. 47
plurale tantum 22, 45
positive 24
posse 20, 21, 26
possessive pronouns 12, 14, 21, 26
prefix 14
preposition 15,16,19,39,43
present tense 24, 26, 30; subj. 39
present stem 33, 34
preterite, past tense, 24, 30

pronoun 13, 14, 15, 18, 26
pudet 35
purpose clause 40, 41

Q
quam, quantus 18
quam + sup. (*potest*) 39
-que 11
questions 9, 10, 11, 17; deliberative41; indirect 41
quis/quī quae quid/quod 18
quis quid indefinite pron. after *sī, num, nē* 34, 44
quis-quam quid-quam 38
quis-que quae- quod- 29
quis-quis quid-quid 43
quod (= *quia*) 20
quot 11

R
reduplication 34, 36
reflexive pronoun 17, 26, 36, 40
relative pronoun 13, 18
result clause 40, 41

S
sē 17, 26
semi-deponent verbs 43
singular 10, 25
sōlus -a -um -īus 30
stem: verbal 14, 18, 23, 26, 34; nominal 19, 21, 23, 27
subject 13
subjunctive 39; pres.39; imperf. 40; perf. 44; pluperf. 45
substantive, noun, 10, 48
superlative 24; *-(err)inus* 29, 38; adv. 29; abs. s. 30
supine 34; s. stem 34
suus/eius 14, 40
syllable, long/short 46
syllabic division 6

T
tam, tantus 18
tense 24, 30, 31, 32
time: abl./acc. 24
timēre nē + subj. 44
transitive verbs 13
trēs tria 11, 28

U
-um gen. pl.= *-ōrum* 44
ūllus -a -um -īus 30
ūnus -a -um -īus 11, 28, 30
uter, uterque 25
ut/nē + subj. 39, 40, 41
ūtī/fruī + abl. 39, 42

V
vel/aut 24
velle 20, 24, 32
verb 12
verse 46
vidērī 38
vīs vim vī 44
vocative: *-e* 14, *-ī* 31
vowels 4